FACING

SUBSTANCE

ABUSE

Discussion-Starting Skits for Teenagers

R. William Pike

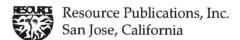
Resource Publications, Inc.
San Jose, California

Editorial director: Nick Wagner
Editor: Kenneth Guentert
Prepress manager: Elizabeth J. Asborno
Copyeditor: Leila T. Bulling

Reprint Department
Resource Publications, Inc.
160 E. Virginia Street #290
San Jose, CA 95112-5876
1-408-286-8505 (voice)
1-408-287-8748 (fax)

Library of Congress Cataloging in Publication Data
Pike, R. William.
    Facing substance abuse : discussion-starting skits for teenagers / R. William Pike.
        p.   cm. — (Acting it out)
    Includes index.
    ISBN 0-89390-374-4
    1. Teenagers—Substance use—Study and teaching (Secondary). 2. Substance abuse—Study and teaching (Secondary). 3. Drama in health education. I. Title. II. Series.
    HV4999.Y68P54   1996
    362.29'071'273—dc20   96-19835

Printed in the United States of America

00 99 98 97 96 | 5 4 3 2 1

Resource Publications, Inc.
160 E. Virginia Street #290
San Jose, CA 95112

Dear Customer,

Due to an oversight, two pages in *Facing Substance Abuse* are missing lines of text. We have provided the corrected pages, which you may glue or tape over the old pages.

Thank you.

Sincerely,

Kenneth Guentert
Customer Service

me that he didn't know what I was talking about. I borrowed the money from my dad that month and told Allan that he better not be wasting our money with his friends.

ELLEN: What did he say to that?

MARSHA: He told me that he wasn't wasting anything and that everything was cool. I opened another bank account, in my name only, just in case. That's when things got bad. First, he started stealing money from my purse. Then he lost his job.

ELLEN: Did you try talking to him about it?

MARSHA: Sure I did.

ELLEN: What happened when you confronted him?

MARSHA: I never really confronted him.

ELLEN: But you just said you talked to him.

MARSHA: Yeah, but he would always storm out and say I was crazy and that I was out to get him. He was getting paranoid about everything. When he took the stereo out of the apartment and pawned it, I knew things were really bad.

ELLEN: What did you do?

MARSHA: First, I moved back home with all my stuff. That's when I realized what he had done.

ELLEN: What do you mean?

MARSHA: When we got engaged, he gave me this beautiful ring. It must have cost him a couple thousand dollars. Because it was so beautiful and because it cost so much money, I used to keep it in a little box in my dresser. (*Getting upset*) When I was cleaning out the dresser, I realized it was gone. He took it and sold it and...

because you have recognized the problem and have decided that you need some help in dealing with it. A few of you are here because a family court judge has decided that counseling for the parent is just as important as counseling for the teenage abuser.

MR. OLDHAM: My daughter's the one who is hooked on crack, not me.

DR. LASKY: I know, I know, Mr. Oldham. And with any luck, we will all help *you* help *her*.

MR. OLDHAM: (*Annoyed*) Whatever.

MRS. GRACE: What is this background information you were talking about, doctor?

DR. LASKY: Well, I usually begin these sessions with some hard core statistics that may amaze you.

MRS. ADAMS: Like what?

DR. LASKY: In my experience, the average parent these days doesn't really know that much about drugs. Kids are getting educated about drugs in school now, but they're getting no reinforcement at home. Parents just don't know the facts.

MR. OLDHAM: What facts?

DR. LASKY: For instance, did you know that a survey of high school kids in 1993 stated that about sixty-six percent of students from grades seven to twelve used alcohol in the past year, twenty-three percent used tobacco, fourteen percent used marijuana, 5.9 percent used hallucinogens, and 2.7 percent used cocaine?

MRS. STREETER: I can't believe that a child in the seventh grade would know where to get cocaine let alone how to use it.

DR. LASKY: Believe it, Mrs. Streeter. The percentage of students may not sound that large, but when

For Chris

Contents

Interpersonal Issues

Legal Issues

Solutions

Introduction

Alcohol abuse, drug abuse, and the dangers of tobacco are topics that have been at the forefront of education in this country for many years. We realized long ago that one of the best ways to help children and adolescents avoid problems with substance abuse was through education. In the past decade, we have attacked these problems with an arsenal of programs, materials, and textbooks. While we certainly have increased awareness in this country, it is distressing to see recent headlines such as "More Teenagers Smoking Cigarettes" or "Young, Carefree, With Taste For Tobacco," or "Crack Mom Gives Birth To Crack Baby!"

Despite all of our efforts, substance abuse continues to be a problem in today's society. The circumstances surrounding substance abuse, however, have changed drastically. Years ago, mothers were not giving birth to babies addicted to crack. Years ago, so-called "designer drugs" were not as popular and widespread. Years ago, tobacco companies were not using cartoon characters to advertise brands of cigarettes. Unfortunately, things have changed.

Consider this fictionalized phone conversation between an irate parent and a suburban high school principal:

PARENT: Hello, is this the principal?

PRINCIPAL: Yes, it is. What can I do for you, Mrs. Allan?

PARENT: Are you aware that James Hersh was just selected as the captain of the varsity football team?

PRINCIPAL Yes, I am.

1

PARENT: Is this the same James Hersh who killed that woman in a car accident last year?

PRINCIPAL: Yes.

PARENT: Wasn't he found guilty of driving while intoxicated?

PRINCIPAL: Yes. It was a tragedy. But how does that concern you?

PARENT: As a member of this community, I am outraged that you would allow someone like that to represent our school and our community as the captain of the varsity football team. What message are you sending to the other students? That it's all right to drink, drive, and kill somebody?

PRINCIPAL: Mrs. Allan, this is a complicated situation. We have been working closely with James and his therapist and we—

PARENT: I don't care about James Hersh! I don't care about his therapist! What about that dead woman? It's wrong that this boy is being honored like this. It's wrong!

Is it wrong?

The details of this conversation have been altered, but the general facts are rooted in truth. The dilemma the parent presents illustrates where today's society stands on the subject of substance abuse. Through education and increased awareness, we know that abuses of this type are wrong, yet we are frustrated at our inability to stamp them out once and for all.

Facing Substance Abuse is the latest weapon in the war against substance abuse among adolescents. This book attempts, as one of the skit characters says, to "put a face" on all the statistics. It presents real problems, real people, and real dilemmas. It challenges readers—both teachers and students— with questions that are not easily answered. It asks them to look at their own behaviors and to examine how those behaviors impact upon their lives and the lives of others.

This book is designed to keep today's teenagers talking about the substance abuse they see in their own lives and in the lives of the people around them. If adolescents are not continually made aware of the dangers of drugs, alcohol, and tobacco, who knows what the headlines will read in a decade or so.

About the "Stage Directions"

This book is designed to be used on an impromptu basis—
without props or preparation—in a classroom and small-group
setting. Detailed stage directions are included mainly to help readers
better imagine the characters, their personalities, and their actions.
When reading the scenes aloud, assign someone the job of reading
all the stage directions. Reading the stage directions aloud will help
the group to grasp the dynamics of the scene and to better understand the information it conveys. Of course, the stage directions can
help organized theater groups prepare more elaborate productions.

Health
Issues

The Spider Web

Topic
physical effects of drugs

Characters
Dr. Joan Armstrong
Dr. Lang
Dr. Jordan

	DR. ARMSTRONG *is conducting a seminar on the effects of drugs on the human body. She is standing at a podium in front of a large screen, lecturing to a group of interns who want to specialize in teenage substance abuse problems in their family practices.*
DR. ARMSTRONG:	(*Getting organized as the audience moves to their seats*) So, how was lunch in the hospital cafeteria? Was it as wonderful an experience as I promised?
DR. LANG:	More so! I actually thought I saw mold growing on the meat loaf!
DR. JORDAN:	You should have asked for a sample to take back to the lab. You might have discovered another strain of antibiotics...
DR. ARMSTRONG:	...or the cause of your heartburn.
DR. LANG:	I decided to "discover" the hamburgers instead. They weren't too bad.

DR. ARMSTRONG: Glad to hear it. Now, let's get back on track. In the morning session, we discussed, in detail, all the specific drugs that today's teenagers seem to be leaning toward. In your practices, you should all be aware of the signs and indications of abuse in these areas.

DR. LANG: But there are so many possible indications. How do we know whether we are diagnosing a problem with crack or with cocaine?

DR. ARMSTRONG: It takes time. And unfortunately, because you will be seeing more and more of people with abuse problems, you will be getting plenty of practice.

DR. JORDAN: That's rough.

DR. ARMSTRONG: It is rough. But, that's not the roughest thing that you are going to confront out there. It is actually easy to recognize the physical effects of substance abuse after you have had some practice. What is really difficult is to try to keep your patients, especially your younger ones, from developing an abuse problem in the first place.

DR. JORDAN: Why should that be so difficult? Once you tell someone about the about all the physical effects of abuse, not to mention addiction, I would think that most sane people would avoid becoming involved in dangerous drugs.

DR. ARMSTRONG: That's just the point. How do you explain addiction? How do you explain dependency? How do you explain the fact that your entire life revolves around getting your next drink, hit, or cigarette?

DR. LANG: Just like that.

DR. ARMSTRONG: It's not that simple, especially when you are dealing with teenagers. Teenagers have a common problem. They think they are indestructible. They think that they are never going to die. They think that "it," whatever "it" may be, won't happen to them.

DR. LANG: What they need is for someone to paint them a picture of the risks of abuse.

DR. ARMSTRONG: Exactly! There are many ways to do that, but the trick is to make it meaningful. Let me show you something. May I have the lights please? (*The lights dim, and the slide of a spider web fills the screen.*) You are all looking at the web of a common spider. You know, those harmless ones you find on your bedroom ceiling. Look at what those little guys can do. The web is an example of architectural genius. Perfectly symmetrical. Wonderfully designed. Completely functional. Beautifully constructed.

DR. JORDAN: That's quite a feat for something your wife only wants you to squish with the sole of a shoe.

DR. ARMSTRONG: Now look at this. (*The slide of a lopsided web comes up on the screen.*) This is the web of a spider that was injected with the equivalent of one marijuana cigarette.

DR. JORDAN: That's what the web looks like after only one joint?

DR. ARMSTRONG: Amazing, isn't it? It has lost almost all of its symmetry and functionality. It's almost as if the spider forgot what he was doing halfway into the task. (*Another image appears on the screen. This web is much worse. There are large holes in its mesh, and it is totally useless as a web.*) What do you think this spider was on?

DR. LANG: Wow. It must have been something intense. It barely looks like a web at all.

DR. ARMSTRONG: This spider was injected with crack cocaine. It's pretty bad, but you can still tell that he was trying to make a web. Now, look at this one. (*This slide shows a web that is absolutely grotesque. It looks like an abstract artist painted his or her interpretation of what a web might look like.*)

DR. JORDAN: That's incredible.

DR. LANG: That's one crazy spider. They must have really pumped that one up with some heavy-duty hallucinogens. What was it, LSD?

DR. JORDAN: Speed? Angel dust?

DR. ARMSTRONG: Caffeine.

DR. JORDAN: I will never have another cup of coffee as long as I live.

DR. LANG: Seriously? All this spider was taking was caffeine?

DR. ARMSTRONG: That's right. But that's not the point. The point of these slides is to provide you with some ammunition.

DR. LANG: Ammunition? What do you mean?

DR. ARMSTRONG: These slides are concrete, physical proof of what certain substances can do to your body and to your mind. These slides are some of the pictures you need to paint for those leery adolescents who think they are immune to the side effects of dangerous substances.

DR. JORDAN: But how can a teenager relate to a spider?

DR. ARMSTRONG: It's simple. A spider's main goal in life is to survive. In order to survive, it must be able to construct webs for food. All the substances we have looked at today impede that construction. Hence, the spider will die as a direct result of using those substances. You have to make the connection that one of our main goals as a species is to survive as well. And just like the spider, we too will die if we can't construct those "webs" we need to sustain life.

DR. LANG: That makes sense.

DR. ARMSTRONG: It's simply a fact of life. Now, let's move on.

Discussion

1. What do you think makes teenagers think they are indestructible or immortal?

2. What happens to the spider's web when spiders are on marijuana, crack, and caffeine?

3. What is the significance of the doctor's findings?

4. How could the doctor's findings about spiders be applied to people?

Two Voices: Dealing

Topic
dealing drugs

Characters
The sister, a twenty-three-year-old girl with a brother who has a drug
  problem
The dealer, a twenty-three-year-old guy who sells drugs to anyone
  with money

>*Both characters speak directly to the audience.*

SISTER: I'm six years older than him. When my mom
went back to work, I had to watch him after
school and take care of him on the weekends.
It wasn't so bad. I mean, he's really a good kid.

DEALER: Hey, man, I got some 'schrooms here. Real
good. Cheap. Did you ever do 'schrooms, kid?

SISTER: When he was twelve, he started smoking
cigarettes. He couldn't smoke a lot back then
because if anyone caught him (meaning me or
my mother) we would have killed him. But I
could smell it on his clothes. My mother
smokes, and I smoke, so I guess it was just a
matter of time. Curiosity. I think that's why he
started in the first place: curiosity.

DEALER: Don't you want to try some? Ain't you the
least bit curious?

SISTER: When he was thirteen, it was wine coolers. They were sweet—like soda. I used to see him and his friends drinking them down at the beach. They thought they were cool. They thought they were all grown up. Soda for thirteen-year-olds. Soda with a kick.

DEALER: If you don't want to do 'schrooms, man, I got some dust. Only ten bucks a bag. It makes you feel like you're floating on a cloud. No kidding. Just ten bucks. Sprinkle some on some pot, and you're flying. Don't listen to all that shit like it messes up your head or that it makes you do crazy things. It all depends on the person, and you look like someone who could handle anything.

SISTER: When he was sixteen, he began smoking pot and drinking a lot of beer. I guess he thought he was a man because there were no more wine coolers around. Only "forties." You know, those big, forty-ounce bottles. That's all he would drink. I used to tell him he was going to have a problem if he kept drinking so much, not to mention all the times he'd come home and throw up in the bathroom. I always had the honor of cleaning it up before my mother got home. All he'd say was that if he drank enough 40s, he would get used to them and wouldn't get sick all them time. I was getting really worried about him.

DEALER: Hey, man, I got just the thing for you. You say you tried everything else? Beer, pot, coke, and you're looking for a new high? Well, it's back. Good old reliable acid. That's right, man. LSD straight from the sixties and right on to this little sugar cube. Go ahead, man, I know you're gonna thank me for it.

SISTER: Yesterday was probably the worst day of my life. It was a turning point, so to speak. I was really scared. This is what happened. It was Saturday night, and my mother was working late, as usual, and I was home with my boyfriend watching a movie on cable. It was about eleven when my brother and one of his friends came busting through the front door. My brother's friend screamed, "Judy, Judy, you gotta help him. He's real strung out." My brother was crazy. He was running all over the house yelling, "I'm scared. I'm scared." I asked his friend what was wrong, and he said he was strung out on acid, and he was having a really bad trip. My brother ran into the kitchen and started screaming that the stove was moving! Then he said he saw a red rabbit jump out of the oven. I didn't know what to do. My god, my brother was so high that he was forgetting to swallow! Finally, my boyfriend and I got him into the car and drove him to the hospital. They kept him a few days, called the cops, recommended a good drug treatment program and released him.

DEALER: So how was it, man?

SISTER: I will never forget that night for as long as I live. And I will never forgive that creep who strung my brother out. If ever I get my hands on him...

DEALER: I haven't seen you around for a while. Is everything cool?

SISTER: We had to tell my mother, of course, and she was furious. "How could you do this to me?" she kept yelling. "I work damn hard for you kids, and this is how you pay me back?" She said that if she ever caught him doing drugs again she would throw him out of the house. I don't know. I understand where she is coming from, but I think she was being a little hard on him.

DEALER: So what can I get for you today, my man? Some dust? Weed? Some more acid? I heard about your bad trip, and I'm real sorry. But you know what they say, if you fall off the horse, the best thing to do is to get back up and ride him again. You're a good kid, and I wouldn't want to lose your business over one bad trip. So here, this is on me.

SISTER: I know my brother. I've just about raised him myself all these years. He's a good kid. He really is a good kid.

DEALER: See ya next week, and hey, you don't gotta thank me for nothing!

Discussion

1. Describe the dealer. What do you think motivates a person like that?

2. Describe the brother. Is it possible that a drug addict could still be a "really good kid"? Explain.

3. What happened when the brother took acid? Do you think that the dealer was right when he said that a bad reaction to a drug "all depends upon the person"?

4. How would your mother react if you had to be rushed to the hospital because of a drug reaction?

5. Do you think that the mother in this scene reacted appropriately? What about the sister's reaction?

6. If this boy were your brother, what would you do to try to help him?

The Parent Group #1

Topic
crack-addicted babies

Characters
Dr. Lasky, the leader of a group of parents with children who are
   substance abusers
Parents in the group:
   Mrs. Adams
   Mr. Oldham
   Mrs. Streeter
   Mr. Meier
   Mrs. Grace

> DR. LASKY *is sitting on a couch in his office with the group of parents seated comfortably around him. This is the group's third meeting, and it has been pre-arranged that* MRS. STREETER *will share her story.* MRS. STREETER *is twenty-five and a recovering crack addict. Her nine-month-old baby was born addicted to crack cocaine.*

DR. LASKY: Welcome to our third meeting, everybody. I don't know about you, but I'm beginning to feel more comfortable here now that I can recognize all your faces and know your names. I sense that the pressures we felt during our first two meetings are beginning to ease a bit. What do you think, Mr. Oldham?

MR. OLDHAM: Maybe. A bit. (*Sarcastically*) But this group will never be at the top of my list of fun things to do.

DR. LASKY: Fun I never promised. The best we can hope for is for each of you to feel that you have learned some things that may help you begin to put your lives back together again.

MRS. ADAMS: I tell you, now that I've already told you all my story, I can sit back and relax. I feel like I've gotten a thousand pounds off my chest.

DR. LASKY: Great. That's really one of the first steps here: to get the "weight off your shoulders," so to speak.

MRS. ADAMS: Well, it works. At least for me.

DR. LASKY: Today, I have arranged for Mrs. Streeter to speak to the group. Before she speaks I would like to fill you in on her background. Is that okay with you, Mrs. Streeter?

MRS. STREETER: Whatever...

DR. LASKY: I'll take that as a "Yes." You see, Mrs. Streeter is a recovering crack addict. She has been clean for almost nine months now, and that's something to be real proud of.

MR. OLDHAM: Why's that?

DR. LASKY: Because crack is so difficult to give up that most addicts need treatment if they are to stop using. You see, crack stimulates the brain's pleasure center, providing a brief but enormously intense high, followed by a plummeting fall. How would you describe it, Mrs. Streeter?

MRS. STREETER: Well, at first, I felt all warm inside. I felt loved, you know? But then you gotta smoke more and more to get that feeling. It starts tearing you up inside. You keep chasing after that first high. At least I did. I kept chasing it and chasing it. But you never do get it back.

DR. LASKY: That "high" disrupts the neurochemical balance of the brain. When it wears off, there is a depressive state that is extreme. In that depressive state, all a person attempts to do is to get more crack in order to repeat the high.

MRS. STREETER: I would have sold my mother to get my crack. I mean it, I would have done anything.

DR. LASKY: After prolonged crack use, a person needs to smoke a good deal in order to just feel okay.

MR. MEIER: Dr. Lasky, I don't mean to interrupt, but this group is supposed to be for the parents of children with drug problems, not for parents who have drug problems *themselves*.

DR. LASKY: You're right, Mr. Meier. Mrs. Streeter, would you like to take over from here?

MRS. STREETER: After I'd been smoking crack for more than a year, I found out I was pregnant. I thought, this shit is killing me, what's it gonna do to my baby? I tried to stop. I really did. But I was just in too deep.

DR. LASKY: Why didn't you go to a doctor or a clinic? Why didn't you seek out some sort of professional help?

MRS. STREETER: I was too afraid.

MR. MEIER: Of what?

MRS. STREETER: I was afraid they were going to try to take my baby away from me if they found out I was a crackhead.

DR. LASKY: I see.

MRS. STREETER: Anyway, the day I went into labor, I was free basing. I didn't even want to go to the hospital, I was so out of it. My husband finally got me into a cab, and we got to the emergency room just in time. I couldn't tell you how the delivery went. Everything was one big blur. All I know is that when they wheeled me down to the intensive care unit for babies, I got real upset. I saw Michael— that's my baby's name, Michael—all hooked up to everything: respirators, monitors, IVs, the works. But the worse thing (*getting upset*), the worse thing was he was making no noises. You could see his mouth moving and his face all scrunched up like he was crying, but no sounds were coming out of him.

DR. LASKY: Michael was born with paralyzed vocal cords, a condition common to babies who are born addicted to crack cocaine.

MR. MEIER: You mean the baby was addicted, just like his mother?

DR. LASKY: Yes. Now do you see why Mrs. Streeter is here, Mr. Meier?

MR. MEIER: My god.

DR. LASKY: Go on, Mrs. Streeter.

MRS. STREETER: When I saw him, he was shaking and jerking around and trying his hardest to cry. When I asked the nurse what was wrong, she said he was going through withdrawal. Oh, yeah, they had to give him a tracheotomy because he couldn't breathe on his own.

The group reacts with feelings ranging from pity to revulsion.

MRS. ADAMS: That's awful.

MRS. GRACE: The poor baby!

MR. MEIER: What a shame.

MR. OLDHAM: The hell it is! It's a crime, that's what it is! This woman should be in prison!

DR. LASKY: Calm down, Mr. Oldham. Mrs. Streeter *was* indeed arrested. At her sentencing, the judge decided that it would do Mrs. Streeter more good to spend the next couple of months with us than behind bars.

MR. OLDHAM: But what she did was—

MRS. STREETER: (*Interrupting him*) Horrible, selfish, disgusting. I agree with you, Mr. Oldham. And believe me, no one has called me worse names than I have called myself.

MRS. ADAMS: How is the baby now? I mean, did he...

MRS. STREETER: They let me take Michael home after about nine months. A nurse stayed with us for the first week. She had to show me how to take care of him.

MR. MEIER: Will he be all right?

MRS. STREETER: The doctors say that with time, he should grow like a normal boy, but he will have his problems.

DR. LASKY: And what about you, Mrs. Streeter?

MRS. STREETER: What *about* me?

DR. LASKY: How are you handling all of this?

MRS. STREETER: Like you said, I've been clean for nine months. I got my job back at the bank.

DR. LASKY: Oh, I forgot to tell everyone that Mrs. Streeter has her master's in business administration.

MR. OLDHAM: And she was a crack addict?

MRS. STREETER: (*To Oldham*) It could happen to anyone, honey. Even you! Like I said, I got my job back, and I got my baby, and I'm trying as hard as I can to do the right thing. Whenever I get even the slightest urge to start smoking rock, I look down at my baby, and I think I've done enough to him. I've got to be strong, now. I have had to sleep in a chair next to his crib at night in case he wakes up and starts to choke, and I swear, you people are my witnesses. I'm gonna be sleeping in that chair until that boy turns nineteen if I have to!

Discussion

1. What is Mr. Oldham's attitude about the group? What could have happened to make him this way?

2. Describe the effect crack has on the brain. How could this effect be dangerous?

3. What is "the neurochemical balance of the brain"?

4. When the "crack high" wears off, what happens?

5. Define "free basing."

6. Describe the problems Michael was born with.

7. Do you think Mrs. Streeter should be in prison? Explain.

The Health Class #1: Substance Abuse

Topic
reasons for abusing drugs

Characters
Ms. Izzo, a health teacher
A few students in the class:
  Mark
  Elsie
  Eva
  Greg

> *The setting is a high school health class. The class has about twenty-five students.* MS. IZZO *is introducing the topic, "Reasons for Substance Abuse."*

MS. IZZO: As we continue our unit on drugs and substance abuse, I want you to make the information that I give you as personal as possible.

EVA: What do you mean?

MS. IZZO: What I mean is that I want you to relate it to your lives in some way.

MARK: Hey, we're not *all* drug addicts, Ms. Izzo.

MS. IZZO: That's not my point. I want you to realize that all of these statistics have faces. It may be the face of someone in this class. Someone in your family. Or someone you just heard about in school. But it's important to see how the concepts we discuss apply to your lives.

GREG: Can you say that again, in English?

MS. IZZO: Okay. Let's take something like self-esteem.

She writes the word "self-esteem" on the board.

I could give you a fancy, scientific definition for "self-esteem," but I want you to be able to relate it to your own lives. So, I'll say that self-esteem affects everything you will do in your life, and it will affect how you grow into adults.

ELSIE: But what exactly is it, and why are we talking about it in the substance abuse unit?

MS. IZZO: Self-esteem is the power to step outside of what feels comfortable and to try something new without worrying about failure. You can look at somebody and see that she or he can take things in stride. There are people who don't let criticism or conflict get them down. People who have low self-esteem think, "I'm no good, so I'm not even going to try." Do you know people like this?

The class emits a general mumble of "Yes."

Can you describe them?

MARK: They lack self-confidence.

MS. IZZO: Good.

MARK: And they don't do very well in school.

ELSIE: Or anywhere else, like at a job or something.

MRS. IZZO: Right. Anyone else?

EVA: They're really unhappy.

MS. IZZO: Yes. And if a person is really unhappy with her or his life, she or he is going to try to escape it somehow.

GREG: You mean suicide?

MS. IZZO: If things are bad enough, yes. But before some people think about suicide, they may attempt to escape the pain they feel by using drugs.

ELSIE: Yeah, they get drunk every night.

MARK: Or stoned.

EVA: It's a quick fix. But what happens the next morning when they're not drunk?

GREG: They have one hell of a headache.

MS. IZZO: And they're right back where they started, with low self-esteem and feeling lousy about themselves and their lives.

MARK: This sounds complicated.

MS. IZZO: It is, Mark. And I don't want to suggest that everyone's problems can be boiled down to a lack of self-esteem. It's not as simple as that. However, esteem problems, especially among teenagers, are major contributors to substance abuse.

ELSIE: So what do you do if you have low self-esteem?

GREG: Is there some pill you can take to make you think you're an okay person?

MS. IZZO: Unfortunately, any pill I have ever heard of eventually wears off, and you are left looking at the same face in the mirror. But there are a few general concepts that counselors believe help combat low self-esteem. I'd like you to write them down.

MS. IZZO *puts each of these ideas on the board.*

First, *communicate.* Ask questions. Talk about your problems. Talk to anybody. Just talk! Second, realize that *you can make mistakes.* No one is perfect, and making mistakes is part of the learning process. Third, *make decisions.* Decide what you want to do and do it. If it was a wrong move, so what? The only real mistake is not learning from your mistakes. Fourth, *deal with conflicts.* Some teenagers don't understand that conflicts are a part of life, and you have to learn how to deal with them. Fifth, *keep your promises.* Sixth, *value differences in others.* Stop putting people down or excluding them. Hating people because they are different usually says more about you than about the person you supposedly hate. Finally, *have a vision for the future.* Have a goal. Dream about it. Then work for it! Because remember, dreams without action wind up as just plain fantasy.

GREG: Slow down, slow down. I'm getting writer's cramp here.

MS. IZZO: I know this is a lot of information, but I wanted you to have it.

EVA: Don't worry about it, Ms. Izzo.

MS. IZZO: Listen, what I am going to worry about is if you just look at these ideas and just memorize them for some test. I want you to think about how they each apply to your life or to the lives of the people you care about. In our next class, we are going to put faces on these terms and definitions, but tonight, ask yourselves this question: "If I have a vision of the future, if I know where I want to be in ten years, why would I want to get stoned every night?" That's the bell. See you all next time.

Discussion

1. What does Ms. Izzo mean when she says that she wants her class to realize that all of the statistics she is presenting have faces?

2. What is Ms. Izzo's definition of "self-esteem"? What is your definition?

3. What role does self-esteem play in substance abuse?

4. Describe a person who has high self-esteem.

5. Describe a person who has low self-esteem.

6. List and define Ms. Izzo's seven ideas for fighting low self-esteem. Do any of them apply to your life? Explain.

Three Voices: Alcohol

Topic
teenagers, alcohol, and depression

Characters
Alice, a junior in college
Jill, a senior in high school
Tim, a ninth-grader
Narrator

> *The four characters are positioned around the stage and speak directly to the audience. The story they tell applies to each one individually; however, it should be spoken as though there is only one speaker. This device underscores the similarities among the lives of many teenage alcoholics.*

TIM: I started drinking when I was...

ALL: ...twelve.

ALICE: I remember that I used to steal vodka out of my grandfather's liquor cabinet.

JILL: I used to mix it in a jar with anything I could get my hands on: orange juice, coke...

TIM: ...Hawaiian Punch.

NARRATOR: If Tim makes it through today without a drink, that means he will have stayed sober for seventeen days. That's pretty significant for a freshman in high school who thinks that he doesn't exist unless he is drunk.

TIM: Look. I'm totally boring when I'm straight.

ALICE: When I'm drunk, I'm a lot funnier.

NARRATOR: Alice has attended four colleges in two years.

JILL: I really am. I mean, at this point, I can't even imagine going to the prom unless I'm loaded. We can't actually drink at the prom, so we're going to have to drink before it starts. They say that the limo drivers are getting wise.

NARRATOR: Jill is the vice-president of her student council.

TIM: When I'm drunk, I can talk to girls. When I'm not, forget it. I don't know. It...

JILL: ...just makes me feel better, that's all.

NARRATOR: Alcohol use by American children has reached alarming proportions. A federal survey of junior and senior high school students showed that at least eight million teenagers use alcohol on a weekly basis and that many of them drink to handle stress.

ALICE: When I was a freshman at the university, I drank between six and twelve beers a night; sometimes I would do straight shots of something. It was a social thing. I guess I was also kinda scared of being away at school.

TIM: I know this kid who died last Sunday of alcohol poisoning. He was fifteen—like me. He went to this party; it was all you can drink for three bucks. Some people said that he had twenty-six shots of vodka. Wow, twenty-six shots.

JILL: When I was a tenth grader, my grades began to suffer because of my drinking, so I decided to only drink on the weekends. What's the problem with that? Last Saturday night, my

friend and I had ten shots of tequila and a half
bottle of champagne, some rum and cokes,
two beers, and that's all I can remember
because I blacked out.

NARRATOR: Many teenagers take part in what is called
binge drinking. Simply put, binge drinking is
drinking enough alcohol to either get drunk or
blackout.

TIM: When I first started drinking beer, it was just
to check it out, know what I mean? I saw
people in these beer commercials drinking—
just the look of it was cool. They were all
having fun. At first...

JILL: ...I was drinking for the taste.

ALICE: By the time I was fourteen, I was drinking...

ALL: ...to get drunk.

ALICE: When I was in high school, we used to play
this game called...

JILL: ..."Power Hour." It was really cool. Each
player had to drink a shot of beer every
minute for an hour.

TIM: Everyone would either get sick or pass out.
The next day, most of us wouldn't remember
what we did the night before.

NARRATOR: It's ironic that while teenagers seem to have a
growing awareness of the hazards of alcohol,
alcohol remains the primary drug of choice
among young people. In addition to all of the
physical and emotional problems associated
with alcohol abuse, there is one problem that
young people don't consider: depression.

JILL: Lately, when I haven't been drinking, I get
really bummed. Worse than usual.

NARRATOR: The combination of alcohol and depression is
a common one.

ALICE: At the end of last year, I transferred to another school. I went to live in the city. I was living in an apartment by myself, and I got really depressed. I got drunk one night, went to a deli, and called my parents. I told them I was going to kill myself.

NARRATOR: In a recent study, sixty-six percent of female alcoholics suffered from major depression. It was seventy-eight percent for male alcoholics.

TIM: When that kid died, I got really scared.

ALL: I thought about how it could have been me. So I stopped drinking. Cold. I didn't think that it was going to be so tough. But, it's been...

ALICE: ...over a year since I had a drink. I'm finding it very hard to stay sober.

JILL: When I decided to stop, I felt like I was the only person in the world who was my age who wasn't drinking or doing drugs. It's been really...

ALL: ...hard.

NARRATOR: You can show a kid genetic surveys and liver enzyme studies and they just don't get it. Recently, Alcoholics Anonymous has been besieged with requests for new materials for teen alcoholics, and across the country, alcohol education is beginning to take place as early as nursery school.

TIM: I know this ten-year-old who is getting off on beer.

ALICE: I saw coloring books about alcoholism for kindergarten kids.

JILL: Hey, folks, better listen up because we all...

TIM: ...got a big...

ALICE: ...problem!

Discussion

1. What does Tim think is wrong with him when he is not drinking?

2. What does Alice think about herself when she is drunk?

3. What killed the fifteen-year-old boy?

4. What is binge drinking?

5. How do you play "Power Hour"? What is the outcome of the game?

6. What do you think is the connection between alcoholism and depression?

7. What do you think is a good age to make children aware of alcoholism? When did you become aware of alcohol? When did you become aware that it can be abused?

The Evening News #1: Smokeless Tobacco

Topic
smokeless tobacco

Characters
Newsperson

> NEWSPERSON *is reading the news into a television camera.*

NEWSPERSON: This just in: Mighty Milton Mossbacher, the legendary major league pitcher and famous pitchman for Dippity Do Dah Chewing Tobacco, has died at his home in Salem, North Carolina. He was fifty-two. Early reports have indicated that the cause of death was acute oral leukoplakia, or cancer of the mouth. According to the American College of Sports Medicine in Indianapolis, there has been a rise in oral leukoplakia due to the increased use of smokeless tobacco—also known as "dip"—by athletes in this country. And, as we all know, Mighty Milton has been selling and using chewing tobacco for years. The American Academy of Pediatric Dentistry has also just announced that in addition to causing various oral cancers and nicotine addiction, chewing tobacco also causes cavities. We are gathering comments from various sports figures who knew and loved Mighty Milton. We will have that for you at eleven. When asked for comment about Mossbacher's death, Amoral Tobacco Incorporated issued this brief statement: "We are all saddened by the loss of this great sports figure. However, we would like to take this opportunity to remind you that there is no scientific evidence linking tobacco products with cancer."

Discussion

1. What caused Mighty Milton's death?

2. What does the statement from the tobacco company indicate?

3. Do you think a major industry would intentionally lie to the general public? Explain.

Sammy

Topic
effect of marijuana on pregnancy

Characters
Susan, a seventeen-year-old girl who has just delivered a baby
Dr. Morrison, the pediatrician assigned to her case

> SUSAN *is lying in a hospital bed. She has just gone through a difficult delivery.* DR. MORRISON *knocks and enters the room.*

DR. MORRISON: May I come in?

SUSAN: (*Still groggy from a local anesthetic*) Uh, sure. Uh, who are you?

DR. MORRISON: My name is Emily Morrison. I am the pediatrician on duty tonight, and I have been assigned to your case. You're Susan Heck?

SUSAN: Yes.

DR. MORRISON: Congratulations, Ms. Heck. You are now the proud owner of a baby boy!

SUSAN: (*Managing a smile*) Is he...is he okay?

DR. MORRISON: (*Trying to ease gently into the conversation*) Are you sure you feel up to talking? We could wait until—

SUSAN: (*Immediately sensing trouble*) What's wrong with him? Tell me, is there anything wrong with him?

DR. MORRISON: Calm down, Susan. He'll be fine.

SUSAN: What do you mean, *will be* fine?

DR. MORRISON: Susan, you know that you delivered almost three months prematurely.

SUSAN: Yeah, I knew it was real early, but tell me what's wrong with him!

DR. MORRISON: His birth weight is dangerously low, and because he was so premature, his lungs have not developed fully, and his eyes are still closed. We have him in an incubator, and we are helping him breath.

SUSAN: (*Getting really upset and beginning to cry*) Oh, god.

DR. MORRISON: (*Letting her cry and then speaking again*) But remember, I said he was going to be fine. If we're careful, you can bring him home in six to eight weeks.

SUSAN: Two months?

DR. MORRISON: That's a possibility.

SUSAN: But he'll be okay?

DR. MORRISON: I think so, yes.

SUSAN: Why did these things happen?

DR. MORRISON: In our experience, there are several reasons why women go into labor early. The one that we see most often is drug use during pregnancy.

DR. MORRISON *sees that* SUSAN *is getting uncomfortable.*

SUSAN: What are you trying to say? That I'm some kind of drug addict or something? Well, I'm not.

DR. MORRISON: Pregnant women do not have to be drug addicts in order to do harm to their babies. Even casual drug use before or during pregnancy can have disastrous effects.

SUSAN: What do you mean by "casual use"?

DR. MORRISON: Well, it depends upon what drug you are talking about: caffeine, nicotine, alcohol, marijuana, cocaine. The list goes on.

SUSAN: What about pot?

DR. MORRISON: Did you smoke pot while you were pregnant?

SUSAN: Yeah, but I didn't think—

DR. MORRISON: How often?

SUSAN: A couple times.

DR. MORRISON: A couple of times during the pregnancy? A couple times a month? A couple times a day?

SUSAN: My boyfriend and I would smoke a couple times a week. That's all. That's not too bad, is it?

DR. MORRISON: (*Trying to be gentle but firm*) Well, I still don't know how much marijuana you actually smoked, but even if it was the equivalent of three or four joints a week during the course of your pregnancy, then yes, Susan, I'm afraid that's dangerous. As you can see by your premature delivery, you did damage to your unborn child.

SUSAN: Oh, god. I didn't know, really, I didn't know. I never would have done anything to—

DR. MORRISON: How old are you, Susan?

SUSAN: Seventeen.

DR. MORRISON: Do you live with your parents?

SUSAN: No.

DR. MORRISON: Your boyfriend?

SUSAN: Yes.

DR. MORRISON: Where is he?

SUSAN: He's at work. They said they called him. He hasn't gotten here yet.

DR. MORRISON: Do you want me to call your parents for you?

SUSAN: No. Not yet. I want to talk to Sammy first.

DR. MORRISON: He's the father?

SUSAN: Yeah.

DR. MORRISON: I hope he gets here soon because you and he have a lot of talking to do.

SUSAN: I know.

DR. MORRISON *begins to leave the room.*

My baby. When can I see my baby?

DR. MORRISON: When you feel up to it, I'll ask one of the nurses to bring you down to the intensive care unit. You'll be able to see him there.

SUSAN: Okay.

DR. MORRISON: By the way, what are you going to name him?

SUSAN: We decided that if the baby was a boy, we would name him after his father.

DR. MORRISON: That's nice. Listen, I have other patients to see. I'll be in later to explain to you and the baby's father what steps we will be taking to make sure that this little guy grows up healthy.

SUSAN: (*Getting upset again*) It's all my—

DR. MORRISON: (*Cutting her off*) There's no time for laying blame now. Right now you need all your strength to help that baby of yours. I'll be back later. And don't worry. I'm going down to ICU to tell Sammy that his mom will be down any minute.

Discussion

1. How old is Susan?

2. What's wrong with her baby?

3. How often did Susan smoke marijuana during her pregnancy? What does her doctor say about this frequency?

4. Do you think that Susan was an uncaring mother? Explain.

5. Do you think that Susan should be held legally responsible for abusing her unborn child? Explain.

Abuse
and
Addiction
Issues

Evening News #2: Smoking

Topic
smoking

Character
Newsperson

NEWSPERSON *is reading the news into a television camera.*

NEWSPERSON: In an alarming announcement, researchers announced today that, while the smoking rates among adults continue to decline, smoking rates among teenagers are on the rise.

The University of Michigan has just concluded a study on teenage smoking that began in 1994. Researchers titled the study "Monitoring the Future." According to one researcher, the future looks pretty bleak. Dr. Eloise Grimsby spoke with a reporter late this afternoon:

"We surveyed fifty thousand students in 1994 concerning their smoking habits. Our results both surprised and upset us. One would think that, with all of the education these days about the link between smoking and all sorts of diseases, kids wouldn't smoke. But, according to our research, more than eighteen percent of eighth-graders, twenty-five percent of tenth-graders, and thirty-one percent of high school seniors said that they had smoked at least one cigarette in the last thirty days. All of these percentages are up by at least one or two percentage points from last year's figures."

When asked why she thought the number of teenagers who smoke continually grows, Dr. Grimsby was a bit vague.

"Our study didn't specifically address the reasons why teenagers were smoking. However, past research has shown that there are many factors that contribute to a person starting to smoke. Several of them are the home environment, peer pressure, and pressure from the media. It seems amazing to me that all of these 'forces' prove to be stronger than the simple fact that if you smoke enough cigarettes for a long enough time you are going to die!"

It is heartening to note, however, that smoking rates among adults have continued to decline yearly.

Discussion

1. What diseases come from smoking?

2. What pressure to smoke is there in the home environment?

3. How does the media provide pressure to smoke cigarettes?

4. Why do you think that teenagers are easy targets for advertisers?

A Definition of Terms

Topic
the criteria for addiction

Characters
Narrator
Teenage Alcoholic

> NARRATOR *and* TEENAGER *are speaking directly to the audience.*

TEENAGER: Hey, I'm no alcoholic. No way. I enjoy a beer every now and then, so what? I'm not hooked on the stuff.

NARRATOR: *(To the audience)* Do you consume the drug in larger amounts than you intended to?

TEENAGER: I like to party a lot. I'm a social person. It breaks the ice. Know what I mean?

NARRATOR: Do you have a persistent desire for the drug? Do you crave it? Have you tried to stop unsuccessfully?

TEENAGER: I just drink on the weekends. Sometimes I get a little too lit but not usually. I know my limits. I would guess that eighty to ninety percent of the kids I know drink just like me.

NARRATOR: Do you spend excessive time seeking out the drug? Would you rather do the drug than do other things?

TEENAGER: And don't tell me that alcohol is a drug. Beer is beer, and drugs are drugs. Any jerk knows the difference. And everybody knows that you can get hooked on some of the shit people are smoking out there. Not on Bud Lite!

NARRATOR: Do you feel intoxicated at inappropriate times? Do you feel any physical symptoms if you don't take the drug for a certain period of time?

TEENAGER: Next they are going to tell me that cigarettes are drugs, too. Come on. Get real. Heroin is a drug. Cocaine is a drug.

NARRATOR: Do you take the drug to relieve or avoid withdrawal?

TEENAGER: Look. Like I said before, it's a social thing. I drink with my friends. We have a few beers. And what's a few beers without a pack of Marlboro?

NARRATOR: Have you felt any of these symptoms for more than a month or repeatedly for a long period of time?

TEENAGER: We are careful when we drink. There is always one person who only has one or two beers. That way we always have someone to drive us home. See, we're not stupid. We don't want to kill ourselves.

NARRATOR: Do you know that different drugs rank differently on the scale of how difficult they are to quit and that nicotine is rated by most experts as the most difficult to give up?

TEENAGER: Both my mom and dad smoke. And they both drink. I was raised that way. What do you want me to do?

NARRATOR: Did you know that addiction is also dependent upon the type of person you are and the specific circumstances of your life? A user may be able to resist dependence at one time and not at another.

TEENAGER: My father said that his father was an alcoholic. He left my grandmother when his kids were real little. My father says he is worried that alcoholism runs in the family, so he's watching how much he drinks.

NARRATOR: Did you know that you can be a casual user of some drugs and still be considered an addict? Some people can only drink one beer a day, but if they *have* to have that one beer, they would be considered an alcoholic. With nicotine, experts believe that ninety percent of smokers are daily users and that fifty-five percent of them are dependent on nicotine.

TEENAGER: If a person drinks every day, he has a problem. If a person went out every Thursday, Friday, and Saturday and got totally blitzed, I would see that as a problem. Right now, I don't think I'm drinking a lot or smoking a lot. Basically, as I said, I'm a social drinker.

NARRATOR: Experts in the field of addiction now say that standard definitions of addiction are too simplistic. As more scientific evidence mounts, definitions are changing. Recently, seven chief executives of tobacco companies testified before a congressional subcommittee that nicotine was not addictive. Ironically, because the definitions of addiction are evolving, experts can see how such a statement might be made.

TEENAGER: Look. I'm a kid. It's the time I should be enjoying life. Now, get off my back.

Discussion

1. From the information presented in the scene, write a list of the criteria for addiction.

2. How would you define the word "addiction?"

3. Do you consider a cigarette to be a drug? Explain.

4. When would a person who has one beer a day be considered an alcoholic? Do you agree that a person who only has one beer a day could be considered an alcoholic? Explain.

5. Do you know any teenagers who may be described as addicted to alcohol or cigarettes? Describe their behavior.

6. Do you think society should "get off the back" of teenagers who drink and smoke cigarettes? Explain.

The Health Class #2:
Marijuana

Topic
reasons for smoking marijuana

Characters
Ms. Izzo, a health teacher
A few students in the class:
  Mark
  Elsie
  Eva
  Greg

> *The setting is a high school health class. The class has about twenty-five students.* MS. IZZO *is introducing the next topic: "Why kids smoke pot."*

MS. IZZO: Okay. I need you all to brainstorm for a minute. Give me a list of all the terms kids use for "marijuana."

MARK: There must be a hundred of them.

MS. IZZO: All I'm asking for is a few.

MARK: What about the age-old word "pot"?

EVA: That's what my dad always calls it. Either pot or grass. Very sixties!

MS. IZZO: What are some others?

ELSIE: A lot of kids call it "herb" or "'erb."

GREG: "Blunts." "Joints."

MARK: "Roaches." "Weed."

MS. IZZO: Good. Good. That's enough. Any ideas why there are so many slang names for "marijuana"?

ELSIE: I never thought about it. But, yeah, it seems that every couple of months somebody is calling it something different. I wonder why.

MARK: Oh, they're just trying to sound cool. It's not cool any more to call it "grass" like our parents did. They want to be different.

MS. IZZO: That sounds pretty reasonable to me. I don't think that anyone really knows why there are so many names circulating out there, but I bet that being different or sounding cool plays a big part in all the slang. Now, what I want to focus on today is the reason why kids *start* to smoke marijuana in the first place. Take a few minutes to think about why. You could also try to remember a marijuana-related story that somehow has affected you. I know that not all of you have tried pot, but I'm sure that you all know people who have.

ELSIE: Ms. Izzo, a couple of weeks ago, my English teacher asked his students to write down, no names of course, if they had ever tried smoking pot. He said that nineteen out of the twenty people in class that day said they had tried it at least once.

MARK: Face it. Half the kids in this school smoke pot every day, and the other half have at least tried it.

GREG: I know a kid who rolled a joint in class once.

EVA: I know somebody who got stoned before a road test. She passed!

MS. IZZO: Unbelievable. Why do you think people smoke?

EVA: This girl said that it calmed her down.

GREG: Numbs the brain is more like it. Pot makes people really moody.

ELSIE: Kids smoke pot because they want to take risks. That's what being a teenager is supposed to be all about, isn't it? "Rebel without a cause" and all that crap.

MARK: Teenagers will never admit it, but it all boils down to peer pressure. If your friends smoke blunts, then you are going to look like a jerk if you don't smoke them, too. So, you smoke blunts. Pressure, plain and simple.

EVA: My cousin was arrested once for smoking a joint at the mall. His father was a detective at the precinct they brought him to. It was really embarrassing.

GREG: In this school, smoking pot and drinking beer are the big things. I'm on the track team, and smoking pot really kills my lungs. So, I just stick to beer.

MS. IZZO: How old are you, Greg?

GREG: Seventeen.

MS. IZZO: And it's easy for you to get beer?

GREG: Are you kidding?

ELSIE: I agree with Mark. Kids smoke pot to be cool. They are pressured into it by other kids. But the pressure is invisible.

MS. IZZO: What do you mean "invisible"?

ELSIE: I mean that you can't see it. Like, nobody is going to say, "If you don't smoke this joint, I'm not going to hang out with you any more." It's not that obvious. If you don't get stoned with a group of kids, after a couple of times they treat you differently. I don't know. It's hard to explain.

EVA: I know what you're saying. They give you looks. Or make comments behind your back. Or stop calling you when there's a party. It's subtle. Real subtle.

ELSIE: But it's pressure.

EVA: People think I'm arrogant because I don't do drugs. They think my nose is always in the air. And you know something? They're right. They're right because I feel I'm better than those dirt bags who do drugs. They don't respect themselves.

MS. IZZO: Self-esteem?

EVA: That's right. And I'll tell you something right now. I respect myself too much to smoke any of that shit!

MS. IZZO: Well, that's sounds like a pretty good place to stop for today. Tomorrow we'll draw some conclusions about what we have talked about.

Discussion

1. Have you ever felt pressured into trying a new drug?

2. How did you respond to the pressure?

3. Why do people feel the need to pressure others into doing what they are doing?

Inexcusable Ads: Dying for a High

Topic
overdosing

Characters
Pitchwoman

PITCHWOMAN *is dressed in a slinky evening dress. Her long blonde hair is flowing over her shoulders, and she is trying to make taking heroin as sexy as possible.*

PITCHWOMAN: (*In a husky voice*) Hey, there. Lookin' for a good time? Well, I've got just the answer. (*Holds up a tiny packet*) See this? This is just about the best time you are ever going to have. It's called DIP. That's right, DIP: Die In Peace. It's the newest, sweetest, purest heroin on the market today. (*She dips her finger into the packet and licks it.*) DIP is actually heroin hydrochloride, and it is ninety-three percent pure. You heard me. Ninety-three percent. That's enough to knock anyone's socks off, honey. Forget what you've heard about overdosing. If you want a ride, you gotta take the risk. But what a ride. You all know that the purity of heroin has been increasing over the last couple of years. In the eighties, it was about forty percent pure. In the early nineties, sixty-five percent. Now, I've been asked to tell you that the magic number is ninety-three percent. So what if the number of deaths associated with our product has increased by thirty-five percent? So what if the Department of Health calls taking our product a form of Russian Roulette? So what? You gotta live a little, don't ya? Or should I say, *die* a little. Come on, be a man. Demand the best. Demand purity. Demand DIP and rest assured that you are going to die in peace. Just look for the skull and crossbones on the package.

Discussion

1. What is DIP?

2. How pure is this particular heroin? Why does the purity present a problem?

3. Why does the Department of Health call this product a form of Russian Roulette?

4. Why would young people try such a deadly drug?

What's My Addiction?

Topic
substance abuse

Characters
Art Adams, host of the television game show
Celebrity panelists:
  Ed Hawke
  Madge Sinclair
  Morty McGinnis
Blunt, the mystery guest addict
Johnny, the voice of the show's announcer

	We are on the set of What's My Addiction?, *a popular game show of the not-too-distant future.*
JOHNNY:	(*Over theme music and a cheering audience*) Hiiii, America! This is *What's My Addiction?*, the game show that's addicting! And now, here's your host, Art Adddddams.
ART:	Thanks, Johnny, and hello, people! Welcome once again to America's most popular TV game show. I'm Art Adams, and for the next thirty minutes, we will all be trying to guess what substance our mystery guest is addicted to. Johnny...
JOHNNY:	This portion of *What's My Addiction?* is brought to you by Bazooka Coolers, the only

wine cooler that's thirty percent alcohol and tastes like bubble gum. Back to you, Art.

ART: Basically, our show is a version of the game Twenty Questions except that our game involves only ten questions. Our three celebrity panelists will ask our guest questions to which he can reply with only a "Yes"or a "No" answer. By narrowing the field of addictive substances and by asking shrewd questions, our panelists will hopefully be able to name the addiction of our guest. Before we begin our game, let's meet our celebrities.

Music plays and the three panelists march out and stand behind a table.

Our first panelist is Madge Sinclair, the well-known TV journalist.

MADGE: Hi, Art.

ART: Our second panelist is Ed Hawke, known to millions as the public watchdog of the tobacco industry.

ED: Art.

ART: And last, but certainly not least, is actor and international action star, Morty McGinnis.

MORTY: Yo.

ART: I would also like to mention that Morty is the founder and chairman of the Morty Center for Drug and Alcohol Rehabilitation.

MORTY: I was my first customer!

ART: We're all proud of you, Morty. Now, is everyone ready to play *What's My Addiction?*

ALL: Sure. Yes. Yo.

ART: Well then, will today's mystery addict please sign in?

From behind the set comes a seventeen-year-old boy. He has stringy hair, a goatee, sideburns, and pants down to his knees. He signs in on the mystery guest board as "Blunt."

ART: (*To the boy*) Is it Mr. Blunt, Blunt Jr., or just plain Blunt?

BLUNT: Are you trying to be funny?

ART: No, I—

BLUNT: Blunt. Just Blunt.

ART: Well, okay, Blunt. Are you ready to play?

BLUNT: Yeah.

ART: You remember the rules?

BLUNT: Uh, no.

ART: These three distinguished panelists will ask you questions—

BLUNT: Oh, wow, there's Morty McGinnis. Hey, Morty.

MORTY: Yo, Blunt.

ART: They will ask you questions. You can only answer "Yes" or "No" to each. Do you understand?

BLUNT: Uh...

ART: Mr. Blunt, do you understand the rules?

BLUNT: Uh, yeah, yeah. I got 'em.

ART: Good. Let's get started. Please set the clock. Ms. Sinclair, first question.

MADGE: Hello, Blunt.

BLUNT: Yeah.

MADGE: Um, Blunt, is your addiction related to needles?

BLUNT: No, man, I hate needles.

ART: Second question, Mr. Hawke.

ED: Do you need to breathe something into your lungs for your addiction?

BLUNT: Uh, yeah.

ART: Continue with the third question, Mr. Hawke, because you received a positive response.

ED: Is your addiction related to something white?

BLUNT: No.

ART: Fourth question, Mr. McGinnis.

BLUNT: Wow, there's Morty McGinnis.

ART: Yes, we've been over that, Mr. Blunt. Try to concentrate on the game.

MORTY: Yo.

ART: Your question, Morty.

MORTY: Oh. Oh. Uh, has your addiction got anything to do with drinking something?

BLUNT: No.

ART: Fifth question, Madge.

ART: Do you do this every day?

BLUNT: Sure.

ART: Continue with the sixth question, Madge.

ART: *More* than once a day?

BLUNT: If I'm lucky.

ART: Is that a "Yes" or a "No," Mr. Blunt?

BLUNT: Uh...

ART: I'll take that as a "Yes." Madge, you're still up. Please ask question number seven.

MADGE: Blunt, you said your addiction is not related to needles or liquid. And you said it's not white. Now, do you eat it?

BLUNT: Uh, you can, but I don't.

ART: That's a "No." Eighth question, Mr. Hawke.

ED: This is getting a bit difficult. Let me see. Does your addiction have anything to do with smoking?

BLUNT: Yeah.

ART: Ninth question and it's still your serve, Ed.

ED: Are you addicted to a derivative of cocaine?

BLUNT: No, man, I stay away from that shit.

ART: (*To his off-camera producer*) Can we take that out of the tape, Jennifer? Mr. Blunt, please watch your language. This is national television, not cable. Mr. McGinnis, you have the last question.

MORTY: Can you grow your addictive substance?

BLUNT: You bet!

MORTY: Art, I'd like to guess. Is Blunt addicted to tobacco?

A loud, ugly buzzer sounds, indicating a wrong answer.

ART: No, I'm sorry, Morty. Unfortunately, he's not addicted to tobacco. And I see that we are out of time and out of questions. Mr. Blunt, would you please tell our panel and our audience what you are addicted to?

BLUNT: Like, I've been smokin' about a half an ounce of weed every day since I was fifteen.

ART: Weed, Mr. Blunt?

BLUNT: Yeah. Weed. Pot. Grass.

ART: Oh, Mr. Blunt is addicted to marijuana. Have you ever tried to stop?

BLUNT: Uh, let me see. I, uh... Totally? Never.

ART: Would you say you are psychologically, if not physically, addicted to smoking marijuana every day?

BLUNT: Yeah, yeah, addicted. I can't let a day go by without smokin' an "L," man.

ART: Well, congratulations on two counts, Mr. Blunt. Because you stumped our panel and because we can clearly see you have a problem with marijuana, you have won our grand prize.

Music plays.

BLUNT: Wow.

ART: Tell him what he's won, Johnny.

JOHNNY: Art, Mr. Blunt has won an all-expenses-paid, two-month stay at the Morty McGinnis Center for Drug and Alcohol Rehabilitation. This exclusive facility has been home to countless stars and sports personalities. And don't forget the "Morty Pledge": If, after your stay at the center, you are not completely drug and alcohol free, you can co-star with Morty in his next action-packed movie. That's all, Art. Back to you.

ART: Thanks, Johnny. Well, what do you say about that, Mr. Blunt?

BLUNT: Uh, you mean I won't be smoking no more weed?

ART: That's right!

BLUNT: No more joints before breakfast?

ART: Guaranteed.

BLUNT: No more being stoned for final exams?

ART: You got it!

BLUNT: I'll have a life? My life?

ART: Absolutely! Aren't you thrilled?

BLUNT: No way, man. Get me the hell outta here. I ain't goin' to no @#$%! facility with some $%&*@ little %&#@* just because you *@$#%...

BLUNT *goes into a tirade, spouting out more obscenities than a family show can handle. Quickly, the theme music swells to drown him out, and the camera goes in for a close-up on* ART.

ART: (*Waving and restraining* BLUNT *at the same time*) Good-bye, everybody. See you next time.

JOHNNY: (*Quickly, over the theme music and credits*) *What's My Addiction?* is taped before a live studio audience, and the producers claim no responsibility for the program's content. This has been a Betty Ford Production.

Discussion

1. What have the panelists been asked to do?

2. What is Blunt's addiction?

3. How can marijuana be addicting?

4. What is Blunt's prize?

5. Is Blunt happy about what he has won? Can you explain why?

6. Do you know any people who display any of Blunt's characteristics?

7. How do you think you could tell a friend that you think s/he has a problem with marijuana?

Dope

Topic
reasons for doing drugs

Characters
Narrator
Jay, a fifteen-year-old drug user

> JAY *and the* NARRATOR *are standing at either side of the stage, speaking directly to the audience.*

NARRATOR: Snow, Flake, Jimson Weed.

JAY: Hey, I'll smoke anything. Know what I mean?

NARRATOR: Ice, Crystal Meth, Crank.

JAY: It don't matter to me as long as I get off. But I know the score. I know what I'm doing. And, to tell you the truth, I know I'm a loser.

NARRATOR: Mescaline, Acid, Space Base.

JAY: I started out like everyone else did, drinkin' beer at parties in junior high and smoking pot whenever we could get some. As I grew up and got into high school, I just kept on smokin' more and more. Then I started tryin' new stuff. You know, all the crap that has a funny name and is real cheap.

NARRATOR: Dust Muffins, Dippers, Special K.

JAY: Like I said, it doesn't matter to me what I do. I went to this party once, and this guy was giving away all this crack. I thought, hell, why not. If the guy is stupid enough to give it away, I can be stupid enough to smoke it.

NARRATOR: Schrooms, Ecstasy, Eve.

JAY: Anyway, this guy was givin' it away because with crack, the first time you get high is the best. But then, after that, you have to smoke more and more. You keep trying to get as stoned as you did the first time. It's nasty, man. That's why I try to stay away from it as much as possible. I mean crackheads are the lowest. They'd sell their own kids to get more crack. It makes 'em real paranoid, too.

NARRATOR: Dust, Space Dust, Hash.

JAY: I knew a guy once who spent more than a thousand dollars one night on crack. A thousand dollars just to kill yourself! Unreal. A couple weeks later I saw him selling hot VCRs and TVs—just like a little kid selling lemonade. Only thing, he was sweatin' like a pig.

NARRATOR: DMT, MDA, LSD.

JAY: But you know what's worse than that? Dust. Angel Dust. Or Dusted Weed. Man, the last time I smoked dusted weed, I lost it. I went crazy. These guys I was with said I kept punching this brick wall. They took me to the emergency room. I broke three knuckles that night. Pretty stupid, huh?

NARRATOR: Peyote, psilocybin, coke.

JAY: I might be stupid, but I'm not too stupid to know that this stuff is bad for you. I know what you're saying: Then why do I keep doing it? Good question. Tough answer. If I really wanted to kill myself, I think I'd just jump off a bridge or something. I don't think that's the reason. I really think that even though I do some pretty stupid things, I'm in control. I'm not like a crackhead or nothin'—selling my parents' VCRs.

NARRATOR: Purple Rain, Lethal Weapon, Crazy Eddy.

JAY: Maybe if my parents gave a shit, I'd stop. But they don't. I know they don't. My sister either. Hey, I got a group of friends that care about me, and when we're hangin' out, we always have a good time. I'm not about to give that up for nothing. Listen, I'm fifteen years old. I can take care of myself! Nothing's gonna happen to me. Trust me.

NARRATOR: Dope.

Discussion

1. Do you think that Jay wants to kill himself? What does Jay think about suicide?

2. Why do you think Jay takes drugs?

3. What does he say about his parents?

4. What do you think about Jay? Do you know anyone like him?

5. If Jay were one of your good friends, what would you say to him about his drug problem?

Voices

Topic
hallucinations

Characters
Three teenagers, the voices of *one* person dependent on crystal
  methamphetamine

> *Three teenagers stand in a straight line and face the
> audience. Even though they speak separately, their
> delivery should give the impression that only one
> person is telling the story.*

1: I stopped.

2: I swear I did.

3: Cold-turkey.

ALL: But they didn't.

1: The voices. Not at first, anyway.

2: When you're hooked on crystals, you don't
   have any privacy.

3: They're always there—always in your head. It
   feels like people are reading your mind.

1: At first, you hear whispering.

2: You can't quite make it out. Then they begin
   to mumble. You don't know what they are
   saying, but you know that...

3: ...they're talking about you.

1: (*Voice*) "Marty."

2: What?

1: (*Voice*) "Marty?"

3: What do you want?

1: (*Voice*) "Watch out for the bugs, Marty."

2: It's called pseudoparasitisis.

3: Big word.

1: (*Voice*) "Watch out for 'em, Marty."

2: It means you think you have parasites crawling on you.

3: Or just under your skin.

1: For me...

2: ...it was always at night.

3: Right when I was falling asleep I'd feel them.

1: Running through my hair.

2: Up under my eye lids.

3: All around my neck.

ALL: Bugs.

1: Of course I couldn't sleep. Once I went without sleep for...

2: ...four days.

3: All from smoking crystals.

1: So I quit.

2: But the voices stuck around for a while.

3: So did the bugs.

1: I panicked.

2: I decided that the only way to make the voices stop was to kill myself.

3: I went up to the roof of my apartment building, and just as I was about to fall over the side...

1: ...this guy grabbed me.

2: The cops saw I was really strung out and brought me to the hospital.

3: The hospital sent me to this treatment center.

1: I've been here a few weeks now.

2: The voices have gotten softer.

3: They tell me that they will eventually go away.

1: But...

2: ...at night...

3: ...I start feeling itchy...

1: ...and I get real scared.

2: Know what I mean?

Discussion

1. Why do people first like using amphetamines?

2. What are some of the side effects of using crystal methamphetamine?

3. Knowing these side effects, why do you suppose people continue to use drugs like these?

Hindsight #1: Smoking

Topic
smoking

Characters
Madge Sinclair, a television journalist and host of *Hindsight*
Ed Hawke, an activist who focuses on the dangers of smoking
Two sixteen-year-old smokers
  Martin Rachel
  Dawn Peters

> MADGE *is interviewing* ED *and the teenagers about the reasons why teenagers start smoking.*

MADGE: *(To the camera)* Good evening, ladies and gentlemen, and welcome to another edition of *Hindsight*, television's most aggressive news magazine. Tonight's first story is really a follow-up to a story we presented two weeks ago. In that story, we interviewed Ed Hawke about the latest studies that have been released about teenagers and smoking. We received so much mail on the subject that we decided to invite Mr. Hawke back, along with two teenagers who are pack-a-day smokers. *(To the panel)* Hello, everyone.

> *They all reply.*

What I want to focus on today is why young
people begin smoking in the first place.
Martin, how long have you been smoking?

MARTIN: Since I was twelve.

MADGE: Dawn?

DAWN: The same.

MADGE: Now, can you two explain exactly why you
smoke?

DAWN: Simple. I like to. It's a social thing, I guess.
Anyway, I want to be a model some day and
smoking burns off a lot of calories. The first
time I tried it, when I was about twelve, I
started coughing, and I thought that it was
really disgusting. I thought I was going to
throw up. I had to learn to like it.

MADGE: Martin, what about you?

MARTIN: My nerves are bad. Smoking kinda calms me
down. It ain't got nothin' to do with the
Marlboro Man or nothing.

MADGE: Do you smoke Marlboro cigarettes?

MARTIN: Yeah, why?

MADGE: No reason. Now, Ed, do you smoke?

ED: No. Never did.

MADGE: Do you have any possible answers as to why
both Dawn and Martin began to smoke at
such a young age?

ED: I have never met these two young people
before, but I can speak in generalities. Several
major studies have just been completed that
indicate that smoking among young people is
on the rise again and Congress is very
concerned about it. Congress is looking at
how tobacco companies are marketing their

products, specifically if they are targeting minors.

MADGE: Ed, I would like to go back to something Dawn said a minute ago. She said that she had to "learn to like" smoking.

ED: Exactly. The tobacco companies spend about five billion dollars a year to convince people that they will like to smoke. In the face of money like that, it shouldn't be so surprising that today's young people seem oblivious to the fact that cigarettes are lethal.

MADGE: Martin, do you have a response to that?

MARTIN: All I can say is that I just heard that they had a cure for cancer, anyway.

ED: That's not true.

MARTIN: I heard that they can just shrink it up and make it go away.

ED: There are some cancer therapies that can help to shrink tumors. But the success of the therapy is limited. It can in no way be considered a cure.

DAWN: I think that if smoking was really so bad for you that they wouldn't be allowed to sell cigarettes in the first place. You go into any drug store, and you see a whole wall of cigarettes behind the cash register. If cigarettes were that bad, why would stores sell them?

MADGE: Dawn, do you think advertising has anything to do with teenagers beginning to smoke?

DAWN: Absolutely not. Kids smoke because either their parents smoke or their friends smoke. It has more to do with peer pressure than with advertising.

MADGE: Martin, do you agree?

MARTIN: Definitely.

ED: The most successful advertising is when people don't think that they are being "pitched to." People need to think that the choices they make in life are their own—that they're not influenced by anything or anyone. Advertisers know this. They're sneaky and they're successful.

MADGE: Have either of you ever tried to stop smoking?

They both shake their heads "No."

MADGE: If you knew someone who was trying to stop, what suggestions would you give?

MARTIN: First of all, you have to realize that you can't tell teenagers what to do. The minute you tell them what to do, they will do just the opposite. That's what being a teenager is all about.

DAWN: If you really want people to stop smoking, raise the price. Make cigarettes five dollars a pack. If people had to spend that kind of money, they would just say, "Forget it."

MADGE: Do you think that either of you will ever try to stop smoking?

MARTIN: Nah, my dad smoked up until the day he died. That's going to be me. We all have to go somehow, don't we?

MADGE: What about you, Dawn?

DAWN: I don't know. Maybe. I'm sixteen now. Maybe when I'm thirty or something or when I have kids.

MADGE: I'm sorry but we are out of time. Thanks very much for sharing your thoughts with us. Maybe some day we'll understand the complex relationship so many people seem to have with tobacco. Until next time.

Discussion

1. Do all of the people whom you see smoking look like they are "burning off calories"? How do they look?

2. What do the tobacco companies spend five billion dollars per year on?

3. Why are cigarettes "lethal"?

4. Presently, is there a cure for cancer?

5. What does Dawn think will make young people stop smoking? Do you agree?

6. Do you know anyone like these young people? Describe them.

Social
Issues

Inexcusable Ads #2:
Mighty Milton

Topic
smokeless tobacco

Characters
Mighty Milton, pitchman for a chewing tobacco company

> MILTON *is speaking directly to the camera in an advertisement that should never make it on television.*

MILTON: Hey, ho everyone! It's Mighty Milton back again to fill you in on the latest about your and my favorite smokeless product, Dippity Do Dah. That's right, ladies and gentlemen, Dippity Do Dah is the best-selling brand of smokeless tobacco in this great nation. Now I hear what all of you are saying out there, "Who in their right mind calls it 'smokeless tobacco' any more?" Well, I'm here to tell you that you can call it whatever the hell you want— "snuff," "spit," or "dip"—just make sure the brand is Dippity Do Dah. Why should you buy this particular brand, you're asking? Well, I'll tell ya! Only Dippity Do Dah provides the sweetest dip buzz you'll ever have. Now, as all my fans know, I haven't been on the mound in quite a few years, but I still remember standing in the middle of that field, listening to the crowd cheering, and putting a humongous hunk of Dippity Do Dah in my mouth for the third inning. The rush I'd get from all that nicotine was indescribable. Only Dippity Do Dah packs its smokeless with so much nicotine that you'll see stars for the first five minutes it's in your mouth. Now seeing stars every time you chew may not be your objective. That's fine. Just spit a lot. Spitting out that juice cuts down your dip buzz just fine. And remember, the ladies just love to see a real man spit. That brown juice running down your mouth will make 'em fall head over heels for you. Now, while we're on the subject of real men, I would like to address one other important topic before my time here with you is up. Everybody knows that Mighty Milton is a real man. Hell, playing in the majors as long as I did would make a real man out of just about anybody. My point is that it takes a real man to chew Dippity Do Dah. Why do I say that? I'll tell ya. I just came from my doctor, and he told me that I have an advanced case of inoperable mouth cancer. You heard me right. Mighty Milton has about six months to live. Doc says it's because I spent all those years chewing on the mound. But, hell, do you see me crying? Do you see me complaining? Have I stopped chewin' tobacco? Hell no! Not Mighty Milton! Why? Because I am a real man. I want to leave this world with the sweet juice of Dippity Do Dah oozing between my teeth. And seeing that this might be the last time I may be speaking with all of you out there, let me leave you with this last thought. I have asked Amoral Tobacco Incorporated (the good people who make Dippity Do Dah) to put this warning on the label of all of their smokeless products: Warning: This product is for use by real men only. Why? Because it takes a real man to look oral leukoplakia in the face and spit! This is Mighty Milton saying for the last time, "Hey, ho everyone!" We'll see you in that great ball park in the sky.

The screen fades to black with the image of Mighty Milton smiling and spitting.

Discussion

1. What does Dippity Do Dah pack its tobacco with? Why?

2. What did the doctor tell Mighty Milton? What was Milton's reaction?

3. How would you have reacted had you been given the same news?

4. Why do you think that Milton chooses not to get upset over the fact that he is dying of cancer?

No Big Deal

Topic
minors buying alcohol

Characters
Four fifteen- and sixteen-year-old students
  Teddy
  Grace
  Micky
  Paul
Mr. Mortimer, owner of a convenience store

> *It's Friday night.* TEDDY, GRACE, MICKY, *and* PAUL *are hanging out in the parking lot of a convenience store and getting up the nerve to go in to buy beer.*

GRACE: I don't care what you guys say. I'm not going to do it.

MICKY: Come on, Grace. It's your turn.

PAUL: Yeah, Grace. I thought we all agreed that we would take turns.

GRACE: I know. But I'm a girl.

TEDDY: Don't pull that "I'm a girl" crap on us again. What does that matter?

GRACE: Well, girls don't buy beer.

MICKY: They sure know how to drink it! Don't they, you guys?

There is a general mumble of agreement and laughter among the guys. GRACE *still doesn't look pleased.*

GRACE: I don't care what you jerks say. I'm not going in.

PAUL: What are you so afraid of, Grace?

GRACE: What do you mean, "What am I so afraid of?" Try getting caught, for one thing.

TEDDY: Old man Mortimer hardly ever proofs anybody. All he wants to do is make money. He doesn't care if you're fifteen or fifty as long as you have cash.

GRACE: Watch. This time he'll proof me.

MICKY: You have that fake ID, don't you? You know, the one you use to get into all the clubs. Those bouncers don't give you any trouble.

GRACE: Yeah, but Mortimer knows my dad, and I think that he could figure out that I'm not twenty-two.

PAUL: Oh, you worry too much.

GRACE: (*To* PAUL) Why don't you go in then, big mouth?

PAUL: Hey, I went in last Friday night. The whole point here is to limit your exposure to getting snagged by spreading around the responsibility.

TEDDY: That's right, Grace. We can't be taking all the risks all the time. If you want to hang out with us, you gotta pull your own weight.

MICKY: Guys, face it. She's too scared that her *daddy* might find out that she drinks brews with the boys on Friday nights.

GRACE: Stop it, you guys.

PAUL: What's the matter, daddy doesn't know that his little angel enjoys a good beer buzz on the weekend? Don't you think he'd approve?

GRACE: I don't care what he knows or doesn't know. I just don't want to buy it because—

TEDDY: (*Nasty*) No more excuses, Grace. It's your turn to go in. If you don't you can forget about drinking with us any more.

The rest of the boys agree. After a pause, the pressure on GRACE *appears to have worked.*

GRACE: Okay, okay, enough with the thumb screws. I'll do it. I'll go in.

PAUL: (*Mockingly*) There you go! That's our little angel.

GRACE: Cut it out, Paulie, or I really will take off, and you guys can dredge up your beer somewhere else.

PAUL: Just kidding, just kidding.

TEDDY: All right. Here's the money. Get three six packs. That should be enough to get us all mildly toasted tonight.

GRACE *takes the money, but she still looks apprehensive.*

GRACE: But what do I say when I go in?

MICKY: Don't say nothing. Just get the beer. Bring it to the counter and give him the money. Keep your mouth closed.

PAUL: Act like you know what you're doing.

TEDDY: Act like you're twenty-two.

GRACE: Yeah, sure, and how does a twenty-two-year-old person act?

PAUL: Who knows? Just get in there. You'll do fine.

GRACE *reluctantly enters the store. She is the only customer. She picks up the three six packs and heads for the counter. She recognizes Mr. Mortimer behind the register. She puts the beer on the counter and takes out her wallet. She decides not to offer Mr. Mortimer the proof unless he asks for it. As he is ringing up the beer, Mortimer keeps looking at* GRACE. GRACE *is sure he is suspicious. She decides that if he asks for ID that she will just run out of the store. When Mortimer turns to speak,* GRACE's *heart is in her mouth.*

MORTIMER: That's $12.75.

GRACE *puts the money on the counter without looking at him or without speaking.*

Outta twenty.

MORTIMER *makes change and bags the six packs.* GRACE *can't believe her luck. He isn't going to proof her. Now all she has to do is get out of the store.* MORTIMER *hands the bag to* GRACE.

MORTIMER: Here you go, young lady.

GRACE: Thanks.

GRACE *takes the bag and turns to go.*

MORTIMER: Oh, young lady.

GRACE *stops and turns. This is it, she thinks.*

GRACE: Yes?

MORTIMER: You're Gene Forrest's girl, aren't you?

GRACE: Yes.

MORTIMER: Say "Hi" to him for me, okay?

GRACE: Sure.

GRACE *turns and walks quickly out of the store to join her friends in the parking lot.*

Discussion

1. Do you think it's easy for minors to buy beer? Why?

2. What do you think should happen to merchants who sell beer to minors?

3. What do you think should happen to minors who get caught buying beer?

4. How would you feel if, as a minor, you were caught buying beer? How would your parents react?

5. Why do you think that Mortimer didn't proof Grace?

Name That Euphemism

Topic
making getting drunk socially acceptable

Characters
Al Martin, the host of the game show
Becky, player one
Doug, player two
Announcer (Johnny)

	Name That Euphemism *is a game show that we all hope we'll never see on television.*
ANNOUNCER:	Hello, everybody, and welcome to another round of *Name That Euphemism*, the game that tests your knowledge of the English language. And now, here's your host, Al Martin.
	The lights go up on the stage to reveal MARTIN *and the two contestants.*
MARTIN:	Hello, panelists. And hello to you folks at home. We have a great show for you today. We also have two great panelists. Let me introduce Becky from New Jersey and Doug from New Mexico. Hi, guys.
BOTH:	Hi.
MARTIN:	Are you both clear about how the game is played?

BOTH: Yes.

MARTIN: Well, for our folks at home, let me briefly go over the rules. We will have three rounds per game. In each round, you will both have sixty seconds to name as many euphemisms you can for the key phrase. In case you didn't know, a euphemism is a polite word that replaces a less pleasant one. For example "ladies room" replaces "toilet" and "environmental engineer" replaces "garbageman." Get the idea?

Both DOUG *and* BECKY *nod.*

Good. Let's get to our first round. Please give me sixty seconds on the clock. You will each have sixty seconds to give me as many euphemisms for the word "drunk." Ready, begin!

The clock begins to tick, and the panelists think for a moment.

BECKY: Tipsy.

DOUG: Tight.

BECKY: Pickled. Soused.

DOUG: Plowed.

BECKY: Stoned.

DOUG: Stewed. Inebriated. Juiced.

BECKY: Three sheets to the wind.

DOUG: Under the table. Lit. Tanked up.

BECKY: Wiped out. Blotto. Plastered.

A buzzer sounds.

MARTIN: Thirty seconds left.

DOUG: Bombed. Buzzed. Polluted.

BECKY: Loaded.

DOUG: Looped. Smashed.

BECKY: Crocked.

A buzzer sounds again.

DOUG: Shit-faced.

MARTIN: I'm sorry, Doug, the buzzer has sounded. Anyway, you know the rules. No vulgarity! And let's tally our first-round scores. After sixty seconds, Becky has named ten euphemisms, and Doug has named thirteen. Doug has won round one. Now, take a break and relax, you guys. When we return, we will try another round. Johnny.

ANNOUNCER: Al, this portion of *Name That Euphemism* is brought to you by Aunt Mary's Kentucky Sunshine, the whiskey that puts a smile on your face and a hum in your belly. Take it from Aunt Mary, we could all use a little more smilin' and a little more hummin'. We'll be right back.

Discussion

1. What does the term "socially acceptable" mean?

2. What's a euphemism?

3. Comment on the name of the product "Aunt Mary's Kentucky Sunshine." Is the name a euphemism? Explain.

4. What term do you commonly use for "getting drunk"? Do you think you use it to make drinking more socially acceptable?

The Session

Topic
peer pressure

Characters
Matt, a community drug counselor
Four teenagers
  Kathy
  Christina
  Joe
  Sean

> MATT *and* FOUR TEENAGERS *are sitting in a large room in the community center. They have been meeting for several weeks in these counseling sessions, and they all feel comfortable with one another.*

MATT: Okay, guys, today I want to focus on the reasons for starting to take drugs in the first place. To begin with, let me throw out the old standby, peer pressure. What do you think?

KATHY: Most kids will say that peer pressure doesn't exist, but it does.

JOE: That's a lot of crap. I don't let anybody tell me what to do. Ever!

KATHY: That's just the point, Joe. Nobody is telling you what to do, but you can still be pressured.

SEAN: It's like it's invisible.

KATHY: Yeah.

JOE: What do you mean "invisible"?

SEAN: I mean it's there, but you don't know it's there.

CHRISTINA: How is that possible?

KATHY: I remember going to this party a couple of weeks ago. I didn't know anybody there, but my cousin dragged me along anyway. There was this girl who came right up to my cousin and said, "Who's this?" My cousin told her, and the girl looked at me and said, "So, do you smoke weed?" I said not any more. Then she said to my cousin, "Then what fun is she?" and walked away. She was trying to pressure me. She wasn't holding me down and forcing me to smoke weed or anything. She was just making it very clear that if I didn't, I wasn't cool, and I wasn't welcome.

CHRISTINA: Yeah. Kids want to be cool. They don't want people to think they're jerks or anything.

SEAN: It all depends on the kids you hang out with.

JOE: Or the kids you *want* to hang out with.

SEAN: What do you mean?

JOE: I mean that some kids will do anything to hang out with a group of people that they think are cool—smoke cigarettes, drink beer, smoke pot—you name it.

CHRISTINA: Those kids are either pretty desperate or pretty stupid.

KATHY: It has nothing to do with being stupid. Even the kids at the top of our class are drinking beer and getting stoned.

MATT: What do you think it has to do with, Kathy?

KATHY: Like I said, peer pressure. Fitting in. Being cool.

JOE: Hey, some of those kids in the calculus class need a few lessons in how to be cool.

SEAN: Yeah, but drinking beer until you puke isn't really necessary.

MATT: Christina, what do you think about all this?

CHRISTINA: I think that getting stoned or drunk is just artificial fun for people who don't know how to be social.

MATT: What do you mean by "don't know how to be social"?

CHRISTINA: I mean that they don't have a lot of friends or they feel awkward in a group of people, so they get drunk to get happy.

JOE: I've seen too many kids on acid, man, and they don't look happy to me. I see them act more crazy than happy.

MATT: Joe, when did you start doing drugs?

JOE: At parties, like most kids. You're there, with all your friends, and someone either pulls out a blunt or a couple bottles of beer, and bingo.

MATT: How old?

JOE: Fourteen. Thirteen.

KATHY: How about trying twelve? When we were twelve, we were getting beers at 7-11, going to parties, and getting stoned.

MATT: What were you doing at fifteen?

KATHY: At fifteen, we were dropping acid. I remember seeing my boyfriend's hands turn into cartoon gloves. You know, like the Smurfs. Everything became like Smurftown.

MATT: What made you finally stop?

KATHY: I was zoning out. I was stoned all the time, and we almost got into this head-on collision one night. That scared me.

MATT: And that was enough to get you to stop doing drugs?

KATHY: It sure was.

MATT: It's scary to think that you almost had to die before you realized what you were doing to yourself. Listen, time's up. Next week, I want you all to think about what got you to stop drinking or taking drugs. Instead of focusing on why we all started, I want to focus on why we all stopped. Think about it. See ya.

Discussion

1. Why is peer pressure invisible?

2. Why are teenagers concerned with being cool?

3. What does being cool mean to you?

4. What does Christina mean when she says that getting stoned or drunk is just artificial fun for people who don't know how to be social?

5. How do you assess your own social skills? Do you ever need the help of drugs or alcohol to feel comfortable in a social situation?

Evening News #3: Tobacco Advertising

Topic
cigarette ads

Characters
Newsperson

NEWSPERSON *is speaking directly into a television camera.*

NEWSPERSON: There has been yet another report about the relationship between young people and the sale of cigarettes.

A California group surveyed five thousand convenience stores in the state and found that the stores located nearest schools displayed more tobacco advertisements than others do.

The study found an average of more than twenty-five tobacco ads and promotions in each store. A spokeswoman for the California group, Liz Asbro, described what they saw. She told reporters, "It was blatant pandering to minors. These people know that selling tobacco products to anyone under the age of eighteen is illegal, yet the stores near high schools and middle schools did a brisk trade in cigarettes. We even found that many of the cigarette ads were placed at the height of three feet or below. Coincidence? I don't think so."

A spokesman for the National Association of Convenience Stores in Alexandria, Virginia, denied the accusation: "That's ridiculous! Our stores and our store owners know the laws, and they abide by them. There may be a few owners who sell tobacco to minors, but they are the exception, not the rule. As for the ads, face it, ads are a part of doing business. Why target convenience stores? Look at all the billboards and ads in the magazines. Look at all the cartoons advertising cigarettes! We feel that the study unfairly singles out convenience stores and their owners, and we demand a retraction!"

The California group responsible for the study refuses to change their claim and still maintains that cigarette promotions were aimed at increasing sales of cigarettes to minors.

Discussion

1. Do you think that convenience stores sell cigarettes to minors frequently or infrequently? Explain.

2. Do you feel influenced by ads in stores to buy cigarettes? Explain.

3. Do you notice more ads for cigarettes in some stores? Do you think their placement is deliberate?

4. Do you think that some cigarette ads are aimed at minors? If so, what do you think should be done about it?

Hindsight #2:
Tobacco Companies

Topic
tobacco companies

Characters
Madge Sinclair, a television journalist and the host of *Hindsight*
Ed Hawke, a political activist who focuses on the dangers of smoking

> MADGE *is interviewing* ED *about a study that he recently uncovered that was conducted by a large tobacco company.*

MADGE: (*To the camera*) Good evening, ladies and gentlemen, and welcome to another edition of *Hindsight*, television's most aggressive television news magazine. Our first story tonight concerns testing a large tobacco company conducted during the seventies and eighties. As you all know, for years the news has been filled with accusations that tobacco companies have known that their products were harmful to the consumers. What did these companies know? When did they know it? And did they continue to sell their products with the knowledge that they were contributing to the deaths of thousands of people every year? To help us answer a few of these questions is Ed Hawke, a man who is known for his quest for truth. Welcome to *Hindsight*, Ed.

ED: I'm glad to be here, Madge.

MADGE: For the past several years, Ed has focused on the tobacco industry. Is that right, Ed?

ED: Yes.

MADGE: Why?

ED: Well, to tell you the truth, Madge, I didn't like what I was hearing. As you said in your introduction, almost every night, it seemed, the news was filled with negative stories about the tobacco industry. And every night would come denials from the CEOs of the companies involved. I decided to try to get to the bottom of a few of those stories.

MADGE: So you began an investigation of your own?

ED: Yes, I did.

MADGE: And what did you find?

ED: I found out a great deal, Madge. Unfortunately, I can't share it all with you tonight.

MADGE: What can you tell our audience, Ed?

ED: I have with me one of the many secret documents I was able to obtain from the research department of a large tobacco company.

MADGE: May I see it?

ED: Of course. (*He passes the document to* MADGE.)

MADGE: This document seems to record a series of tests that the company conducted.

ED: Exactly.

MADGE: What was the subject of these tests?

ED: One of the tests was conducted in the 1970s and concerned hyperactive third-graders from Virginia.

MADGE: What would a tobacco company want with hyperactive third-graders from Virginia?

ED: It seemed that the company tracked these children into adulthood to see if they used cigarettes later in life to calm down.

MADGE: Wouldn't that imply that cigarettes may have a narcotic effect on people?

ED: I would think so.

MADGE: And when you are talking about narcotics, aren't we really talking about drugs?

ED: In some cases, yes. What's your point?

MADGE: My point is, Ed, doesn't this information indirectly say that the tobacco industry was treating their product as though it were a drug?

ED: (*Smiling, having already drawn that conclusion and pleased that others conclude the same thing from the research*) Why, yes. I suppose it does.

MADGE: Do these documents reveal anything else, Ed?

ED: It seems that this tobacco company conducted research on college students from 1969 to 1972.

MADGE: What sort of research?

ED: Electroshock.

MADGE: What?

ED: According to this data, electric shocks were administered to college students to see if their smoking increased under stress.

MADGE: Did it?

ED: The results were inconclusive.

MADGE: This is unbelievable.

ED: Not really.

MADGE: What do you mean?

ED: Do you really expect a major company not to test its product to see the effects it has on the consumer?

MADGE: No, I...

ED: It's perfectly acceptable to conduct tests such as these, Madge. After all, the more you know about something, the better off you are.

MADGE, *smelling a rat at first, finally gets* ED's *point.*

MADGE: What you are saying is that the tests themselves aren't what's at issue. The issue is that the companies involved knew, and have known, the results of tests like these for years.

ED: Exactly. It appears from these documents that certain companies have viewed tobacco as a drug for many years and that, from extensive testing, they know a hell of a lot more about its impact on the consumer than they want *us* to know.

MADGE: Aren't they obligated to tell us?

ED: Legally, all they are required to do is print those warnings from the Surgeon General on the side of each pack.

MADGE: Haven't you made the discovery of these tests public recently?

ED: Yes. I brought my findings to a member of Congress, and yesterday morning she held a news conference.

MADGE: Have you had any response from the tobacco company involved?

ED: They just issued this statement this morning. (*He holds up a piece of paper.*)

MADGE: Please read it.

ED: All it says is, "We have always said that we have studied why people smoke."

MADGE: What they fail to add is that they have also withheld their findings from the public.

ED: Hey, Madge, grow up. That's how you do business in this day and age.

MADGE: And with that, we have to go to a commercial break. Thank you for coming on, Ed.

ED: My pleasure.

MADGE: When we come back, we will speak to a woman who was one of the first thalidomide babies of the fifties. She is now in her mid-forties, and it appears that thalidomide is making a comeback.

Discussion

1. In your opinion, why do millions of Americans smoke cigarettes?

2. What is the narcotic effect smoking has?

3. If tobacco companies view their product as a drug, why don't they warn smokers?

4. Do you think the government should intervene? Explain.

5. Knowing that tar and nicotine are classified as drugs, would you start smoking or continue to smoke?

Evening News #4: Marijuana

Topic
marijuana use among teenagers

Characters
Newsperson

> NEWSPERSON *is speaking directly into a television camera.*

NEWSPERSON: Another federally funded study concerning the connection between young people and drugs has been concluded. This time the government wanted to track the use of marijuana among high school students. According to the new study, in 1994, marijuana use among young people increased for the second straight year.

A spokesperson for the government said, "The percentage of high school seniors who have tried the drug increased from 35.5% in 1993 to more than 38% in 1994. This increase follows a more-than-decade-long *decrease* from the highs of the 1970s. No pun intended."

The spokesperson went on to explain that in 1979, for example, 60.4% of all high school seniors indicated that they had smoked marijuana at least one time.

The study provided no reasons as to why marijuana use is increasing.

Discussion

1. Can you offer an explanation for 60.4% of all high school seniors smoking marijuana in 1979?

2. Why do you think there was a rise in marijuana use in 1994?

3. What do you think makes marijuana such a popular drug for young people?

4. Can you think of any ways to discourage more young people from trying the drug?

Inexcusable Ads #3: Zing!

Topic
glamorization of drinking

Characters
Three twenty-something guys
Voice
Announcer

> THREE TWENTY-SOMETHING GUYS *who look like they have jumped out of an MTV promo zoom up to the beach on three jet skis. They push their jet skis up on the beach, take off their life jackets, and collapse on the sand.*

1: Wow!

2: Awe-some!

3: Great!

1: I didn't think that the waves were so big. But when we got out there, I caught some great rides.

2: Yeah, I saw you get bounced off your machine a couple times.

3: Yeah, but the ignition kicked off as soon as I fell off.

1: Good thing—or else you would have been swimming home and chasing a runaway jet ski.

2: (*To* 1) I took a beating out there too! What did you bring to drink?

3: I hope that you didn't bring beer again.

1 nods that he did bring beer, and the other two guys react with incredulity.

3: Hey, don't get us wrong, we love beer. After all, we've been drinkin' it since we were eight. All we're saying is that we just got a taste for something different.

All of a sudden, from out of the blue, a VOICE speaks from out of the heavens. The THREE GUYS look up and listen.

VOICE: Are you looking for something different?

All three nod.

Are you looking for something to replace that boring taste of beer?

All three nod.

Then open your minds and open your mouths to the great taste of Zing!

Three bottles of Zing! drop into each of the guys' hands.

ALL: Wow!

VOICE: Go ahead. Try a taste. Zing! comes in three great tastes. Grape...

1 takes a swig and smiles.

VOICE: ...orange...

2 takes a swig and smiles.

VOICE: ...and tutti-frutti.

3 *takes a swig and smiles.*

VOICE: Each of these new flavors is the result of endless taste tests! These are the flavors *you* kids like the most, so these are the flavors of new Zing! What do you think?

1: Wow!

2: Awe-some!

3: Great!

VOICE: I thought you'd like them.

All three guys drain their bottles and react as if they were mildly drunk.

(*Noticing their reactions*) Oh, I can see that you are feeling the effects of Zing! already. You'll be pleased to know that unlike beer, Zing! is nearly fifty percent alcohol. So that when you taste that smooth, fruity flavor, you are actually getting a sizable buzz!

ALL: Cool!

1: Can we have another?

VOICE: Sure.

From the sky, three more bottles drop into their hands. The boys quickly open them and begin to guzzle.

Have as many as you like because Zing! will not show up on any breath-alizer devices, either. No one can spoil your fun now!

ALL: Cool!

The guys finish their drinks, throw the empty bottles on the beach, and run off for their jet skis. Just as they are about to zoom off, the voice says...

VOICE: Hey, don't forget your life jackets!

The guys pause for a moment, look at each other, say, "The hell with it," and race off.

VOICE: (*After a warm chuckle*) Kids today! (*To the audience*) You might forget your life jackets, but never forget your Zing! Zing! in three natural fruit flavors. Put some zing into your life. Try one today!

The picture focuses on the three guys driving wildly and erratically through the waves. They all seem to be smiling and oblivious to any danger as the announcer comes on. The announcer speaks so fast that his message is all but incomprehensible.

ANNOUNCER: Zing!containsfiftypercentalcoholbyvolumeand isconsideredanalcoholicbeverage. Saleto anyoneundertwenty-oneyearsofageisforbidden bylaw.

The music swells as the boys race off.

Discussion

1. What made the three young men ride off without their life jackets?

2. What was the result of putting some zing into the lives of these three guys?

3. How does the advertising world always portray its product?

4. Can advertisers be irresponsible? Explain.

Interpersonal Issues

Three Worlds

Topic
dealing

Characters
Amy, the girlfriend of a dealer
Phil, a sixteen-year-old who deals in school
Mr. Santi, a high school principal

> *Each character is speaking directly to the audience.*

AMY: Have you ever gone out with a guy who deals drugs? Let me tell you, it's no picnic.

PHIL: Yeah, so, I deal. What's the problem? I just do it for spending money and to pay the car insurance. That's it. Nothing big.

MR. SANTI: I hate to admit it, but yes, we have kids in our school who sell drugs. We have kids who deal in the community, and we have kids who deal at school. The community is the police's problem. This school is my problem first, and then it becomes a problem for the police.

AMY: This might sound stupid, but a major pain was that when I beeped him, he never called back. He always said he was too busy. He always said he was with his friends. His friends. What a terrific bunch they are.

PHIL: Your friends will either make you or break you. You gotta network, if you know what I mean. You gotta have your people tell other people who tell other people about you. That's the only way you are going to make any money. You just have to hope that the wrong people don't find out.

MR. SANTI: We know who they are. The tough thing is to prove that they are involved in drugs. Some of these guys, *and girls*, think that we have no idea what they're up to. They think that other kids don't tell us what's going on. How can they be so naive? Don't they know that the teachers are aware of their behavior? Don't they know that people see them going off behind the gym during lunch?

AMY: The worst thing about it was that his friends are always "dropping by," if you know what I mean. Whenever we were alone at his house on a Friday night or if we were watching a movie at my house, people constantly interrupted us. People on the phone. People at the door. People wanting to get stoned. People wanting you to get stoned. It was too much.

PHIL: At school, the first thing you learn is not to keep anything in your locker. Your locker is the first place they look. Whatever happened to private property, anyway?

MR. SANTI: If we suspect something, the first thing we do is check the student's locker.

PHIL: So, what I usually do is put the stuff in my girlfriend's locker, or, if she isn't cool, give the stuff to one of my friends.

MR. SANTI: We don't usually find anything there.

PHIL: What I like to do is to put it in my sock. That way you have it on you, and you can get rid of it fast if you have to.

MR. SANTI: They usually carry it around if they plan to sell it that day, so sometimes we have to search them. We ask them to empty their pockets and take off their socks. Can you believe it? A lot of them keep it in their socks! It's a hassle.

PHIL: It's a real hassle when one of the principals takes you down to the nurse to search you. I keep yelling, "This is unconstitutional! You're violating my rights!" That's just to keep 'em off balance a little.

AMY: Before we broke up, he got called in by the principal for dealing. They actually brought him down to the nurse and searched him. It was real embarrassing. Not for him—he thought it was cool—but for me! All my friends kept asking me why I was going out with a jerk like that. I told them I loved him. They told me to get a life.

PHIL: A couple weeks ago I had a close call.

MR. SANTI: A couple of weeks ago we had an interesting case. We were told that this boy, whom we had suspected was dealing in school for quite a while, was going to sell a couple joints to another student in the boys' room during fourth period.

PHIL: I was going to sell three joints to this kid I didn't know. Usually, I have to know about the kid before I do a deal. Anyway, I needed the money, so I got sloppy. I agreed to meet him in the bathroom halfway into fourth period. Well, the bell rang at the beginning of fourth and the principal and two of his honchos pull me out of class.

MR. SANTI: When we took him out of English, I could tell by the look on his face that we surprised him.

But as he was getting out of his seat, I thought I saw him put something in his mouth.

PHIL: Well, when I saw them at the door, I went to my socks and stuffed those babies into my mouth, fast. I was still chewin' as they brought me to the nurse.

MR. SANTI: He swallowed the evidence before we could nail him.

PHIL: I was so stoned by the time my father picked me up I didn't know what was happening.

AMY: That was it. This kid was going to mess up his life, but I sure wasn't gonna let him mess up mine. The day he swallowed the joints, I could tell that someone had gone through my locker. That meant that they thought I was involved in all of this, too. Because I was his girlfriend, I was into dealing. That's when I dumped him.

MR. SANTI: The next day, Amy, his girlfriend, came to my office. She was very upset that someone had gone through her locker. I told her that under certain circumstances, a principal has the right to go through a student's personal belongings. But that wasn't what she was upset about. She said she was upset because we thought that she was dealing. She told us that she just broke up with him and that she never was and never will be involved in selling drugs. I told her I was glad to hear it.

PHIL: Wow, the worst thing was that my girlfriend ditched me after that. But that's okay; she was getting to be a pain anyway. There are plenty of other women out there, especially for a guy who can throw around as much money as I can. She's the loser, not me.

MR. SANTI: Phil knows now that we are keeping an eye on him, so he's going to be really careful about the business he conducts in school. With any luck, maybe we made him think twice about selling drugs for a living, especially at sixteen.

AMY: He'll never change. I know it. Anyone who uses pot like an after-dinner mint will be a loser all his life.

PHIL: Hey, a man's gotta do what a man's gotta do. Right? Like I said, she's the loser, not me.

Discussion

1. Do you think a principal should ever involve the police when dealing with a student? If so, when?

2. What does Phil mean when he says he hopes that the wrong people won't find out?

3. Would you ever turn in a student for dealing drugs at school? Explain.

4. Explain Amy's problem with Phil's "friends."

5. Should a principal have the right to search a student for drugs?

6. Do you think Phil will ever change? Explain.

The Parent Group #2

Topic
the role of siblings in encouraging abuse

Characters
Dr. Lasky, the leader of a group of parents with children who are
  substance abusers
Parents in the group
  Mrs. Adams
  Mr. Oldham
  Mrs. Streeter

> DR. LASKY *is sitting on a couch in his office with the group of parents seated comfortably around him. This is the group's second meeting.*

DR. LASKY: (*Looking around*) Well, I see that everyone decided to come back for another round.

MR. OLDHAM: What choice do we have?

DR. LASKY: Oh, yes, Mr. Oldham, I forgot. Some of you have been ordered by the court to attend these sessions. Don't worry, it'll go fast. You might even learn something while you're "serving your time."

MR. OLDHAM: I doubt it. What am I going to learn from someone's sob story?

DR. LASKY: You would be surprised. But before we begin, let's just review some of the ground rules.

Remember, at each meeting we are going to share some of our personal stories concerning our kids and their experiences with drugs or alcohol. Also, at each meeting I will try to give you all some information regarding the current situation of substance abuse in this country today. Your stories will appeal to our hearts, and my information will appeal to our intelligence. Maybe, by combining both our hearts and our minds, we can solve a few of your problems.

MRS. ADAMS: Dr. Lasky, do you still want me to go first?

DR. LASKY: Sure, Mrs. Adams. Do you think you're up for it?

MRS. ADAMS: I think so, but where should I start?

DR. LASKY: Wherever is easiest for you.

MRS. ADAMS: Okay. I've been married for seventeen years, eighteen this coming June, and my husband and I have—had—two boys: Jason, who just turned sixteen, and Billy, who would have been fourteen next month.

MRS. STREETER: Why do you say "had"?

MRS. ADAMS: (*Beginning to get upset*) Let me work up to that part, okay?

MRS. STREETER: Sure, sure. Take your time.

MRS. ADAMS: We were always your typical "Brady Bunch" family. Both my husband and I worked, and our boys always did well in school. We went on vacations in the summer, and every couple of years we would make it to Florida over Christmas vacation, like everyone else. The boys were inseparable. Wherever Jason went, Billy was right behind. Billy would do whatever Jason did, even though he was two years younger.

DR. LASKY: What happened when they got older?

MRS. ADAMS: When the boys got older, they both developed their own circle of friends, but Billy still always looked up to Jason. If Jason listened to a certain new band, Billy would have to listen to them. If Jason got an ear pierced, Billy would have to have his pierced, too. I really didn't think it was a problem until...

DR. LASKY: Until when?

MRS. ADAMS: Until I noticed some changes in Jason.

DR. LASKY: What changes?

MRS. ADAMS: He started to hang out with a different bunch of kids. He said he was bored with the friends he grew up with and that he had more in common with this new crew. They were tougher. More street-wise, if you know what I mean. And they were into drugs.

DR. LASKY: How do you know they were into drugs?

MRS. ADAMS: I don't know. You can just tell sometimes. The jokes they make, the clothes they wear, the music they listen to. I don't mean to stereotype any kids, but when it's your own kid, you just seem to know.

MRS. STREETER: How does Billy fit into all of this?

MRS. ADAMS: Well, when Jason hung out with this new friends, his little brother, of course, wanted to hang out with them, too. For some reason, Jason didn't mind Billy trailing him around. Last year, this new group that the boys were listening to announced a concert tour. Jason bought tickets, and Billy wanted to go with him. My husband and I decided that Billy was too young to go without an adult. There was a big blow-up, but we held to our decision. Jason went with his friends, without his brother. Billy finally forgot about the concert, and everything got back to normal. That is, until two months ago when the group announced another tour. This time we couldn't stop Billy from going with his brother.

DR. LASKY: What happened at the concert?

MRS. ADAMS: (*Getting upset*) We thought we had nothing to worry about. If Billy got into trouble, we knew that Jason was there. Jason would never let anything happen to him. They were such good kids, bright, athletic...

DR. LASKY: If this is too difficult for you, Mrs. Adams...

MRS. ADAMS: No, no, I'll be fine. It's just that it only happened a few weeks ago.

DR. LASKY: I understand. Take your time.

MRS. ADAMS: At the concert, it seems that all the kids were doing some kind of drugs. I don't know. I forgot the name, and Billy did the drugs, too. Everything was fine at the concert, but on the way home they decided to stop at Grisham Lake. Someone had the bright idea of going for a midnight swim. They all went into the lake, and Billy never came out. The police had to drag the lake for his body. I don't know if I should blame Billy or Jason or the drugs or myself. All I know is that my little boy is dead and I...

MRS. STREETER *goes over to comfort* MRS. ADAMS. *All of the parents in the group, including* MR. OLD-HAM, *are visibly moved.*

DR. LASKY: Why don't we end it there for tonight? But just let me say that a situation like this could creep up on any family. The world kids live in today has some significant differences from the world we were brought up in. Careers change every five years; the mass of information doubles every three years. Today there are designer drugs that are almost instantly addictive. They are cheap, and they are twenty times stronger than those used ten years ago. We're going to learn that there are many things we can do as parents to avoid tragedies such as this, but the first thing we have to realize is that something like this could happen to any family. Once we all know that we are vulnerable, we might be able to do something to protect ourselves and our children. Thanks, Mrs. Adams. I'll see everyone next week.

Discussion

1. What is Mr. Oldham's attitude toward group therapy?

2. Would you join such a group if you thought it would help you or a member of your family? Explain.

3. How did Jason encourage Billy's abuse?

4. Do you think that Jason caused Billy's death? Explain.

"Your Parents Are the Greatest"

Topic
parents as enablers

Characters
Sean, a graduating senior
Sean's parents
  Mr. Becker
  Mrs. Becker
Wayne, Sean's best friend, also a graduating senior

> SEAN *and* WAYNE *are sitting at the kitchen table of the Becker home. They will be graduating from high school in less than a month, and they have a serious problem: no one has planned a graduation party yet.*

SEAN: Are you sure Grace said she wasn't going to have it?

WAYNE: Positive. She said her parents said, "No way! Not again!" Don't you remember what happened at her last party?

SEAN: Barely. I was so drunk I don't remember much of anything about that night.

WAYNE: Her house was totally trashed. They had to call the cops because of the fight on the front lawn, and Grace said that the next day she had to carry garbage bags of vomit out of her house.

SEAN: Not pretty.

WAYNE: I can't blame her folks.

SEAN: Neither can I. Parties around here have gotten pretty wild lately. Everybody gets so stoned and drunk that they don't know what they're doing.

WAYNE: Are you speaking from experience?

SEAN: Listen, I may get drunk, but I don't get crazy. Give me some credit.

WAYNE: Okay. Okay.

SEAN: But that still leaves us with our original problem.

WAYNE: Yeah. Where? Hey, what about here?

SEAN: We just had that big party over Christmas vacation.

WAYNE: And it was one of the best parties all year.

SEAN: I know, but the way things are going with people's houses getting trashed...

WAYNE: Your parents were cool last time, weren't they?

SEAN: Yeah, but...

WAYNE: They didn't hassle you about the beer, did they?

SEAN: No, they were pretty cool about it.

WAYNE: So, what do ya say? Ask 'em.

At that moment, MR. BECKER *and* MRS. BECKER *come in from food shopping. They put the bags they are carrying on the table and look at the boys.*

MRS. BECKER: Why the long faces?

MR. BECKER: It looks like you two just came home from a funeral.

WAYNE looks at SEAN as if to say "Go on. Now's the time to ask."

SEAN: Wayne and I were just working out a little problem.

MRS. BECKER: What's wrong, honey?

SEAN: Ya see, nobody wants to have a graduation party after the graduation ceremony.

MR. BECKER: What? No party? (*Intentionally overblown*) Why that's un-American!

MRS. BECKER: Why not?

WAYNE: (*Carefully concealing the truth about the damage done at past parties*) Uh, everyone is just too busy—what with the prom and everything.

MR. BECKER: Too busy to have a party to celebrate perhaps the most important event of your young lives?

WAYNE: That's what they said.

MRS. BECKER: What about that nice girl who lives over on Penny Street? What's her name?

SEAN: Grace Pauley.

MRS. BECKER: Grace, that's right. Doesn't she have a nice house for a party?

SEAN: (*Under his breath*) She *had* a nice house for a party.

MRS. BECKER: What's that?

WAYNE: Uh, she just had one a couple of weeks ago, Mrs. Becker.

SEAN: Yeah, and—

WAYNE: (*Cutting him off before he can add the details*) And she's just too busy.

MRS. BECKER: Well, why don't we have it here?

SEAN: Mom, I—

MR. BECKER: That's a fine idea. You kids shouldn't be deprived of a little fun after all your hard work!

SEAN: Dad, you don't understand.

MR. BECKER: Nonsense! I understand perfectly.

MRS. BECKER: (*To her husband*) And so do I. It's a wonderful idea, Murray.

SEAN: But there are going to be kids drinking again.

MRS. BECKER: Well, kids will be kids.

MR. BECKER: That's right. Can't do nothing to stop teenagers getting beer, can you?

MRS. BECKER: And I'd rather have you two drinking at home rather than at somebody else's house.

SEAN: But what if somebody gets into an accident or something going home? Aren't we responsible?

MR. BECKER: No one will get into anything. If you think someone is too drunk to drive, just let me know and I'll drive him or her home.

WAYNE: That's real nice of you, Mr. Becker.

SEAN: But, Dad...

MR. BECKER: No buts about it. It's settled. You boys draw up the specifics and let us know.

SEAN: But...

MRS. BECKER: (*Kissing her son on the top of the head*) It will be fine, dear. Listen to your father.

> MR. BECKER *and* MRS. BECKER *leave the kitchen, thinking they have done their son and his friends a great service.*

SEAN: I can't believe you.

WAYNE: (*Patting him on the head, mocking his mother*) "It'll be fine, dear. You'll see." (*Laughs*)

SEAN: Listen, you better make sure it *is* going to be all right.

WAYNE: What do you mean?

SEAN: You better make sure that nobody trashes this house!

WAYNE: No problem.

SEAN: And you are going to dump out all the garbage bags full of—

WAYNE: Okay. Okay. I get the picture. Hey, Sean, who's going to buy the beer?

SEAN: I don't know. Don't you have that fake ID?

WAYNE: No. My dad took it away from me. Wait a minute.

SEAN: What?

WAYNE: I got it. We'll ask your dad to buy it.

SEAN: You gotta be kidding!

WAYNE: No I'm serious. Your parents are the greatest. Watch.

> WAYNE *runs off in search of the Beckers.* SEAN *runs after him.*

SEAN: Wayne. Wait a minute, Wayne…

Discussion

1. What is an "enabler"?

2. Are Mr. and Mrs. Becker aware of the fact that they are enablers? Explain.

3. How are they helping to create a disaster?

4. Do you know any enablers?

5. Do you think you were ever an enabler yourself? Explain.

Priorities

Topic
parental use of marijuana

Characters
Alison, a sophomore in high school
Meg, Alison's good friend

ALISON *and* MEG *are in the high school cafeteria.*
ALISON *is obviously angry over something.*

MEG: Hey, Alison, could you believe that biology test? He never told us that we had to know the complete life cycle of the Great American Bull Frog.

ALISON: (*With an attitude*) Yes, he did.

MEG: No, he didn't! I would have remembered!

ALISON: Face it, Meg, you failed the test because you didn't study! Don't blame it on the life cycle of the Great American Bull Frog.

MEG: Hey, what's up with you today? I can always count on you to back me up when I'm trying to shift the blame. What's up?

ALISON: I'm just really pissed, okay?

MEG: At me?

ALISON: No, no.

MEG: At who?

ALISON: Who else? My father.

MEG: Not him again? What did he do this time—pawn your stereo?

ALISON: No. It was Becky's birthday a couple days ago.

MEG: Oh, right, I forgot. How old was she?

ALISON: Nine.

MEG: Wow, I remember when she was born! What did your dad do, forget all about it or something?

ALISON: No.

MEG: Then why are you pissed? Come on, Alison, talk!

ALISON: I made sure he remembered. A week before her birthday I told him it was coming up and to make sure that he got her a present.

MEG: So he didn't get her a present?

ALISON: Yeah, he got her the new Elton John CD. He said, "Sorry it's only a CD, but money's kinda tight."

MEG: So what's the problem? He got your sister a present. It's not much, but if money is tight, what can you do?

ALISON: That's just the point. I don't understand how he can spend so much money on some things and next to nothing on things that are really important—like me and my sister.

MEG: What are you talking about?

ALISON: Last night Jimmy came over.

MEG: You mean that guy who sells your dad the pot?

ALISON: Yeah. And do you know what my father did? He gave him $450 in cash!

MEG: Wow, he's really into it!

ALISON: And I have a real problem when he says that he's tight for money and then three days later spends it all on his drugs.

MEG: Does your sister know?

ALISON: No. And don't tell her, either. She has enough to deal with.

MEG: I know he's your father and all, Alison, but that guy is a real jerk. How long has he been smoking so much pot?

ALISON: Well, he's been smoking as long as I can remember, but lately, it's been getting real bad. I can remember when I was little that I always wanted to stay at school. I never wanted to go home. Becky's like that now. She is on every after-school club or team you can imagine. She's told me that it's almost painful for her to go home after school.

MEG: You're the same way. You were always staying after school, and now you have that job at Burger King. You must get home after ten at night! Is it all because your father smokes so much dope?

ALISON: That's a big part of it. Before my mother left, they would always fight over his smoking. Real loud. Real nasty. After about five minutes, my dad would say, "You girls go upstairs and play." That meant they were really going to duke it out. Now, whenever Jimmy comes over, my dad uses the same line, "You girls go upstairs and play." Now it means he is going to get stoned.

MEG: How do you know?

ALISON: Haven't you noticed that everything in our house has this sweet, smoky smell? The curtains. The couch. My clothes! After a while, the smoke travels up to my bedroom and I know...

MEG: That's a rotten way to live.

ALISON: You get used to it. But I've been doing my best not to let it get to Becky. I don't want her to get as messed up as I got over this.

MEG: You're not messed up, Alison, you—

ALISON: Listen, I'm only fifteen years old. My mother left us when I was eight, my sister and I hate to go home, I have to be both father and mother to my kid sister, and my father is a drug addict! I call that pretty messed up.

MEG: I know it's rough and everything, but can you really be addicted to pot?

ALISON: I know they say that there is no real physical addiction. But come over to the house sometime and check out my father. If he's not addicted, I don't know who is.

MEG: I suppose the last thing on your mind was passing that biology test.

ALISON: I'm trying to keep up with school, but my father is making it harder and harder. I wish he'd just get his priorities straight.

MEG: What do you mean?

ALISON: I just wish he'd realize that his two daughters are more important than smoking a joint.

Discussion

1. Describe Alison's family situation. What do you think about her dad?

2. Would you consider her father's drug use a form of child abuse? Explain.

3. Do you think that Alison and Meg may become involved with drugs? Why or why not?

4. Define the word "priorities." How does that word apply to Alison's situation.

5. Do you know any parents who use drugs? Do their children know? How does it affect their family life?

The Engagement Present

Topic
substance abuse and relationships

Characters
Ellen, a family counselor
Marsha, her twenty-year-old patient

> *The scene takes place in* ELLEN'S *office.* MARSHA *has been seeing* ELLEN *once a week for about a month.*

MARSHA: (*Knocking on a partially open door*) Hello. Anyone home?

ELLEN: Hi, Marsha. Come on in. Hey, that's a great haircut. When did you get it done?

MARSHA: (*Taking a seat, self-conscious about her new hair style*) Yesterday. Yesterday afternoon.

ELLEN: It looks great. What made you cut it so short?

MARSHA: I don't know. I needed a change, I guess.

ELLEN: Well, it's definitely a change for the better.

MARSHA: Thanks.

ELLEN: Where do you want to start today?

MARSHA: (*Still a bit uneasy with the therapy*) I don't care.

ELLEN: Last time you told me about Allan's cocaine use. Do you want to pick it up from there?

MARSHA: Sure.

ELLEN: How frequently was Allan using cocaine?

MARSHA: First off, it wasn't really coke. It was crack. He was smoking crack. I know that they are sorta the same thing, but, let me tell you, crack is worse.

ELLEN: In what way?

MARSHA: Well, first off, it's cheaper than coke. Allan could never have afforded to smoke as long as he did or as much as he did if it were cocaine. Second, crack is nastier.

ELLEN: What do you mean?

MARSHA: I mean, have you ever met a crackhead before?

ELLEN: No, I haven't. At least I don't think I have.

MARSHA: Oh, you would know it if you had. All crackheads are the same. They want one thing out of life and one thing only—more crack. It takes over their lives. Totally.

ELLEN: Where would Allan get the money to buy it?

MARSHA: Right after we got engaged we moved into an apartment together. We both had good jobs, and we could pay the rent and the car payments with no problem. After a couple months, I noticed that we were getting short on money at the end of the month. I knew Allan used to get stoned with his friends on the weekends, but I didn't realize that things were getting so out of hand.

ELLEN: What do you mean that things were getting out of hand?

MARSHA: Well, three months ago we didn't have the rent money. We were both still working and everything, but the money just wasn't in the checkbook. I asked Allan about it, and he told everything, but the money just wasn't in the checkbook. I asked Allan about it, and he told me that he didn't know what I was talking about. I borrowed the money from my dad that month and told Allan that he better not be wasting our money with his friends.

ELLEN: What did he say to that?

MARSHA: He told me that he wasn't wasting anything and that everything was cool. I opened another bank account, in my name only, just in case. That's when things got bad. First, he started stealing money from my purse. Then he lost his job.

ELLEN: Did you try talking to him about it?

MARSHA: Sure I did.

ELLEN: What happened when you confronted him?

MARSHA: I never really confronted him.

ELLEN: But you just said you talked to him.

MARSHA: Yeah, but he would always storm out and say I was crazy and that I was out to get him. He was getting paranoid about everything. When he took the stereo out of the apartment and pawned it, I knew things were really bad.

ELLEN: What did you do?

MARSHA: First, I moved back home with all my stuff. That's when I realized what he had done.

ELLEN: What do you mean?

MARSHA: When we got engaged, he gave me this beautiful ring. It must have cost him a couple thousand dollars. Because it was so beautiful and because it cost so much money, I used to keep it in a little box in my dresser. (*Getting upset*) When I was cleaning out the dresser, I

ELLEN: (*Calming her*) It's okay, Marsha, it's okay. It's good to cry about it. What did you do then?

MARSHA: Well, I didn't see him for a couple of weeks, almost a month. Then I heard from one of his friends that he was in the hospital.

ELLEN: Because of the crack?

MARSHA: Well, not exactly. I guess Allan got into a fight with some guys who said he owed them money, two thousand dollars or something. Allan got crazy. He started screaming and punching the side of a building with his fists. He kept punching and punching until this guy jumped on him trying to make him stop. Then...

ELLEN: I know this is rough for you, Marsha. You don't have to—

MARSHA: No, I have to finish the story. Then Allan's father showed up. Somebody called him. He grabbed Allan to try to calm him down. That's when one of the guys who said Allan owed him money pulled out a gun and shot Allan's father in the back. He said, "This is just a warning."

ELLEN: Did the police ever come?

MARSHA: Yeah, finally. They found Allan holding his father, rocking back and forth. All he would say was, "It's too late. It's too late." He was right.

ELLEN: Who was?

MARSHA: Allan. It was too late.

Discussion

1. What drug was Allan using?

2. What did Marsha notice after a few months of living with Allan?

3. What is the significance of Allan selling the engagement ring? How would you react if that happened to you?

4. Why was Allan's father shot?

5. What did Allan mean when he said, "It's too late"?

6. Explain how Allan's drug use affected the relationships he had with the people in his life.

Legal
Issues

The Evening News #5: Alcohol Psychosis

Topic
alcohol psychosis, serving alcohol to a minor

Characters
Newsperson

> NEWSPERSON *is speaking directly into a television camera.*

NEWSPERSON: Last night, a thirteen-year-old girl was struck by a train and killed as she sat on the tracks with a group of her friends.

Kim Sun Phong, a ninth grader, had gone to the popular hangout with a group of friends after attending a neighborhood party. Several witnesses said that Kim Sun had been drinking at the party and was drunk when struck by the train.

Jessica Smart, Kim's close friend, was with her on the tracks when the accident occurred. "We were all just sitting on the tracks and talking. Some of us had had a lot to drink at the party. Kim was drinking a lot of beer. She was pretty lit. Anyway, Kim was spinning around with her arms out on the tracks pretending she was a bird. She kept spinning and spinning and saying, 'I'm untouchable. I'm untouchable. I'm a bird. Look at me fly.' We all heard the train coming and got off the tracks. Just as it was about to pass us, Kim jumped up on the tracks. Nobody had time to do anything to help her. After the train passed, I turned around and looked for her, but she was gone. All I saw was blood everywhere."

Another witness to the accident, fifteen-year-old Walter Gross, told authorities that Kim was drunk. "She didn't know what she was doing. I've seen her at other parties, and she didn't usually drink anything. But tonight was different. I guess she just wasn't used to it. She was only thirteen."

Kim's older sister, Jan, told authorities that Kim was recently going through a difficult time at home. The family moved to the United States from South Korea when Kim was seven. It seems that Kim had a difficult time adjusting to the move. It also appears that Kim's parents had a difficult time adjusting to our culture as well. Jan said, "Last summer, my father caught Kim smoking cigarettes. He got very angry. He told Kim that she was being influenced by the wrong people. He decided to send Kim back to South Korea for the summer to live with my grandmother. When Kim got back, she was really quiet. She was a good kid. I don't know how something like this could happen."

Sergeant Hammond from the homicide squad added, "At this time, we do not think that this was a suicide. We believe that it was an accident brought on by intoxication. The engineer of the 9:10 out of the city said it took him about a mile to bring the train to a stop after the accident. He will not be charged with a crime. Witnesses at the scene said that one second Kim was there and then nothing."

Funeral services for the thirteen-year-old girl have not yet been announced.

Discussion

1. Describe how Kim got the alcohol she drank. Have you ever known this situation to occur?

2. Why were Kim and her friends on the tracks in the first place?

3. Describe how Kim was struck by the train. How did she allow this to happen?

4. Define "alcohol psychosis."

5. Describe Kim's family life. What part do you think this played in her drinking beer?

6. Do you think that the adults who were serving the beer at the party are in any part responsible for Kim's death? Explain.

The Evening News #6: Alcohol Abuse

Topic
supplying alcohol to minors

Characters
Newsperson

> NEWSPERSON *is speaking directly into a television camera.*

NEWSPERSON: Do you remember last week when we reported the tragic death of thirteen-year-old Kim Sun Phong? Well, today, there is an interesting follow-up to the story.

As you recall, Kim was struck and killed by a train after allegedly becoming intoxicated at a neighborhood party. Today, police officials have announced the arrest of Adam Rojas, the thirty-two-year-old host of the party where Kim was allegedly drinking.

Captain Alan Parker told reporters, "We have been investigating this case ever since the accident occurred last Thursday night. It seems that Rojas was hosting a party at his home at which alcohol was being served to people under age twenty-one. A guest at the party saw Kim drinking beer there. We arrested Rojas today and are holding him on $4,000 bail."

Meanwhile, neighbors of Rojas have said that he usually has been a good neighbor. Kate Perry, who has lived next door to Rojas for more than ten years, explained that it was not unusual for Rojas to be around young people. "He likes to teach the kids how to play sports. He and his son, Danny, are always playing basketball in the driveway with a bunch of kids. He's a nice guy, except when he's drinking, that is. After he has a few beers, he changes. He becomes nasty."

Rojas was charged with two misdemeanors: endangering the welfare of a child and first-degree unlawfully dealing with a child. Rojas could receive up to a year in jail on each charge.

In a related story, a judge in New Hampshire ruled today that the family of a twenty-year-old man who died in a car accident following a Halloween party last year can sue the hosts of the party for damages because they served him alcohol even though he was only twenty at the time.

New Hampshire officials have said that "adults don't fully understand that they can be held legally responsible for serving alcohol to a minor."

Alice Gray, a member of a New Hampshire chapter of Mothers Against Drunk Driving commented, "Adults should be aware! I know that every year we get a dozen or so complaints about alcohol being served at sweet sixteen parties. Adults don't have to actually physically give alcohol to a minor. If it's there and it's available, then that's enough. The adult is legally bound."

Gray continued to say that if you are going to serve alcohol, you have to be responsible because she believes that "alcohol is a loaded weapon."

Discussion

1. How old is Adam Rojas?

2. Why was he arrested?

3. With what crime was Rojas charged?

4. What should adults realize about alcohol, minors, parties, and this law?

5. Do you think this law is fair? Explain.

Inexcusable Ads #4: The HDT

Topic
home drug testing

Characters
Pitchman

> PITCHMAN, *dressed in a suit and tie, is speaking directly to the camera and is attempting to sound as respectable and authoritative as he can.*

PITCHMAN: I am not really a doctor, although I play one on TV. But the people at HDT have convinced me to speak to you about the benefits of their newest line of HDTs. Now I know that you are all familiar with the home drug tests for marijuana and alcohol. How many of you applying for that job at the post office have first used one of these products before your interview? It's nice to know that all questionable substances are out of your system before you get asked any embarrassing questions. And millions of you have used our HDT for marijuana prior to your physicals for military service. You were all confident that all traces of THC were out of your urine before Uncle Sam began to stick his nose where it doesn't belong. And we have heard from thousands of airline pilots thanking us for our HDT for alcohol. You guys have a tough job, and it's nice to know you can relax with a martini or two before that trans-Atlantic flight. Who ever said that alcohol impairs your ability to fly a DC-10, anyway? Well, today, I am here to tell you about our new line of HDTs. Because the pressures in our society grow so quickly, new drugs and illegal substances are always flooding the market. Let's face it, as long as there are people, there are going to be drugs. And as long as there are drugs, there is going to be HDT! To keep up with these changes, HDT announces its home drug tests for cocaine, crack cocaine, amphetamines, and LSD. You heard right: HDT is expanding. We are now offering a full line of home drug tests for the latest mind-altering substances. Now, for the first time ever, you can enjoy cocaine in your home, and when it's time for that random drug test at work, you can check to see if it's completely out of your system before they do. How safe! How fast! How convenient! Hey kids, big test tomorrow? Do some acid the night before and the next morning use our HDT for LSD to make sure there's no trace of it left in your body in case the teacher decides to send you down to the nurse! What a breakthrough! Remember, don't let anyone infringe on your civil liberties! Your urine is your own business! And, even though I only play a doctor on TV, I can safely tell you all to go out and buy the HDT of your choice today!

Discussion

1. If companies are allowed to perform drug tests, shouldn't a person be allowed to perform them at home?

2. Do you think drug testing will prevent drug use? Why? Why not?

3. Do drug tests at work or at school infringe upon a person's privacy? Explain.

Hindsight #3: Drug Dealers

Topic
drug dealers

Characters
Madge Sinclair, a television journalist and host of *Hindsight*
Dr. Locks, an urban drug dealer

> MADGE *is interviewing* LOCKS *about his life's work.*

MADGE: (*To the camera*) Good evening, ladies and gentlemen, and welcome to another edition of *Hindsight*, television's most aggressive news magazine. Tonight, it is our pleasure (*uncharacteristically scattered*)—well, it's not really our pleasure, but in any case, we're glad he's here. Well, we're not really glad. We're—oh, anyway, Dr. Locks, welcome to *Hindsight*.

LOCKS: Thanks, I think.

MADGE: Let's begin by asking you about your name. Where did "Dr. Locks" come from?

LOCKS: It's like this. Look at the hair, man. Look at the hair.

> LOCKS *has long, black dreadlocks pulled into a ponytail.*

It's kinda like my trademark. If you know what I mean.

MADGE: Oh, the dreadlocks! I see. You say it's your trademark. Your trademark for what?

LOCKS: What do you mean?

MADGE: I mean, what is your line of work?

LOCKS: You want to know if I sell drugs. Is that what you're asking me?

MADGE: Well, I... Yes, yes, I suppose that is what I'm asking you.

LOCKS: Look. Things are always the same in the city. Everybody is either buying or selling something. It don't change, and it don't really matter what end you're on. We're all just trying to survive, if you know what I mean.

MADGE: I'll take that as a qualified "Yes."

LOCKS: Listen, is this just between us?

MADGE: Of course.

LOCKS: Maybe I move a little merchandise once in a while. So what? I don't have no choice. You gotta make a living.

MADGE: Aren't there other ways to make a living? Legal ways?

LOCKS: Look. Hustling drugs is tough, man, partly because crack prices are down.

MADGE: Why's that?

LOCKS: Because there's so much shit out there it's not worth anything.

MADGE: Why else is hustling drugs tough from your perspective, Mr. Locks?

LOCKS: The police is out there now.

MADGE: Haven't they always been out there?

LOCKS: Yeah, but they don't slap you around any more just to mess with you. They want arrests.

MADGE: I've read that the police in this city have forced many low-level dealers, like yourself, off the streets.

LOCKS: That's right. And it's damn tough doing business indoors.

MADGE: Why?

LOCKS: A man who's buying is jittery, know what I mean? He don't want to go into no record store or nothing. He wants to score and take off. It makes it tough. I'm not making the money I used to.

MADGE: (*Sarcastically*) I'm sorry to hear that. About how much are you used to making?

LOCKS: When I used to be on the street, selling right off the corner, with my pockets full of stuff, I used to make $2,500 a day, easy. No middle men. No runners. No overhead. Nothing. Just you and the customer. Those were the days.

MADGE: Are kids still getting involved in dealing?

LOCKS: Hell, yeah.

MADGE: Tell me about that.

LOCKS: The kids are crazy today, man. There are thirteen-year-olds out on the street making serious money. I'm talking about a grand a day right in their pockets. I'm an old man compared to them.

MADGE: How old are you?

LOCKS: Hell, I'm twenty-eight. These kids are making money hand over fist, and they're spending it just as fast.

MADGE: What about the police?

LOCKS: If these kids get busted, they're out the next day.

MADGE: Why's that?

LOCKS: Because they are so young. Ain't nobody gonna keep no thirteen-year-old kid behind bars long.

MADGE: How do these kids wind up?

LOCKS: They wind up one of two ways. Either they move south with a fat bank account when they grow up or...

MADGE: Or?

LOCKS: Or they don't grow up at all. It ain't no joke out there.

MADGE: I'm not laughing, Mr. Locks. On that note, let's go to a break. When we return, we will meet a thirteen-year-old dealer who claims he has $200,000 in the bank.

Discussion

1. Why does Mr. Locks think that his job is difficult? Do you agree with him? Why shouldn't he be complaining?

2. How much money could Mr. Locks make on the street? Are you surprised by that figure? Explain.

3. What is the fate of thirteen-year-old drug dealers? Do you feel that the risk is worth it? Explain.

A Sobering Thought

Topic
automatic license suspensions for DWI arrests

Characters
Judge Wood, a state judge
Tim Taylor, the defendant
Agnes Rogers, the defense attorney

TAYLOR *has been arrested for driving while intoxicated. He is now being arraigned before* WOOD.

WOOD: Mr. Taylor, you are being arraigned on the charge of driving while intoxicated. How do you plead?

TAYLOR: Not guilty, your honor.

WOOD: Very well. I will set your court date for Tuesday, the fourteenth.

ROGERS: Thank you, your honor.

WOOD: Ms. Rogers, as you are aware, this state has recently passed a law stating that if a person has been arrested for driving under the influence of alcohol, at the arraignment his or her license will be automatically suspended. Therefore—

TAYLOR: (*Interrupting*) But, that's not fair!

WOOD: (*Surprised and slightly taken a back*) Excuse me, Mr. Taylor?

ROGERS: What my client is saying is that he believes this law is unconstitutional and if you impose it we will claim double jeopardy at sentencing.

WOOD: Mr. Taylor, do you understand what your attorney has just said?

TAYLOR: Yes, your honor. If you take my license away today and then find me guilty and sentence me on Tuesday the fourteenth, you will be punishing me twice. Punishing a person twice for the same crime is double jeopardy.

WOOD: Very good, Mr. Taylor.

ROGERS: Furthermore, your honor, I would like to bring up the point that my client is presumed innocent until his trial. By suspending his license today, at arraignment, you are assuming he is guilty as charged.

WOOD: Ms. Rogers, I do not consider the suspension of a driver's license a punishment. I consider it a measure of protection for other drivers on the road who are not intoxicated.

TAYLOR: But, Judge, you haven't given me enough time to make other arrangements if you take away my license today.

ROGERS: You haven't even given my client a meaningful hearing. He needs to present the circumstances of his arrest, and you need to review them before you take away his license.

WOOD: Please do not tell me what I need to do, counselor. We all need to abide by the law. And this state considers the suspension of a license at a DWI arraignment to be *civil* in nature. That means, Mr. Taylor, suspending your license is not a *criminal* punishment. Therefore, no double jeopardy statutes will be

broken if Mr. Taylor is found guilty and
sentenced under our penal code.

TAYLOR: So, what you're saying is that by taking away
my license now, you are not punishing me?

WOOD: Correct.

TAYLOR: What else would you call it? (*Getting upset*) I
haven't even been found guilty of anything
and you have the right to—

WOOD: Calm down, Mr. Taylor. You may apply for a
hardship license which entitles you to drive to
and from work and family emergencies only.

ROGERS: But—

WOOD: No buts, Ms. Rogers. You client's driving
privileges are hereby suspended. I will see
you both back here on the fourteenth. And,
Mr. Taylor...

TAYLOR: Yes, your honor?

WOOD: I hope you have a ride home.

Discussion

1. What are your feelings about automatic license suspensions for
   DWI arrests?

2. What does the term "double jeopardy" mean?

3. What does the judge consider the suspension?

4. What does Mr. Taylor consider the suspension?

5. In your opinion, who is correct? Explain.

Evening News #7: Pregnancy and Drug Abuse

Topic
pregnancy, drug abuse, and the law

Characters
Newsperson

NEWSPERSON *is speaking directly into a television camera.*

NEWSPERSON: Yesterday, in Seminole County, Florida, a woman was accused of delivering illegal drugs to a minor through her umbilical cord. Twenty-three-year-old Joyce Mirabella was found guilty of having violated Florida's drug-trafficking statute by giving birth to a baby who tested positive for a cocaine derivative. Mirabella, a known drug user, was cautioned during her pregnancy by Medicaid officials to refrain from drug use.

Alice Thomkins, a doctor at the clinic, told reporters that she was well aware of Mirabella's case. "This is her third child. In the past, we always suspected drug use, but this time she admitted her problem when she came in during her first trimester. We told her that she would be hurting her baby if she used drugs, and we also told her of the new statute concerning pregnant women. I guess she just couldn't kick her habit."

The doctor who delivered Mirabella's baby said that Mirabella admitted to cocaine use the morning she delivered the baby. Dr. Greenspan said, "When she was in labor, she told me that she had smoked some crack that morning. I told her that we would talk about it after the delivery. After the baby was born, we ran a few blood tests, and both the baby's blood and the mother's blood tested positive for cocaine. By law we were required to turn the results over to a child protection investigator. As I understand it, they notified the police."

Johnson could be sentenced to jail time or community control. Officials have said that others in these types of cases rarely go to jail. They usually must attend a drug rehabilitation program, remain employed, get a general education degree, and abstain from drug or alcohol use.

Ms. Mirabella is due to be arraigned tomorrow. We'll keep you posted.

Discussion

1. How did the baby receive the drugs?

2. What type of drug was it?

3. What did Mirabella do on the morning of her delivery?

4. Do you think that Mirabella should be punished by the law?

5. Name some alternatives that could be used in place of punishing Mirabella.

6. List some ways to prevent pregnant woman from using drugs.

Solutions

Boot Camp

Topic
instilling responsibility

Characters
Sarge, the group leader, a drug counselor
Four teenage "recruits"

> *The scene takes place in the near future at a detention center for adolescent substance abusers. The state has decided that if you are eighteen years old and have been arrested three or more times for a drug-related crime, you are mandated by the court to serve a minimum of three months and a maximum of one year at "boot camp." The scene opens on the first day for four new "recruits." They are standing in line, in an open field. SARGE is pacing back and forth shouting instructions.*

SARGE: All right, listen up and listen up good! You four are my property for at least the next three months and, if you don't behave yourselves, I could stretch that to the next twelve months. Let me tell you something at the get-go. This ain't no summer camp.

1: No sh—

SARGE: (*Not allowing him to finish the statement*) Enough! You will never speak until you are spoken to. Is that clear?

1 *does not respond.*

I said is that clear?

Again, no response.

I'm talking to you now, so you can open your mouth and speak. Is that clear?

1: I guess so.

SARGE: Fine. And another thing. If I hear even one word that strays from the King's English, we are going to have a problem. (*To the group*) Is that clear?

The group mumbles "Yes."

Fine.

SARGE *begins to pace again and look around the field.*

Now, let's get a few things straight. Do you all know why you're here? (*Pointing to* 2) You! Why are you here?

2: Because the only other place they'd let me go was back to jail.

SARGE: Excellent! I want you all to understand that. If you weren't here, you'd all be in jail right now. Three strikes, and you're out. Sound familiar? Because you are all eighteen or younger and because you have all been arrested not once, not twice, but three times, the judicial system has decided that this is the best place for you.

1: That's a load of sh—

SARGE: (*Again bellowing an interruption*) You again! You get one more warning. You either watch your language, keep your mouth shut, and do what you're told, or you're back on the road crew cleaning the state highways for five hours a day! Understand?

1: All right. All right. Chill.

3: This guy means business.

SARGE: I most certainly do mean business. This is what is known as your last chance. This is your last shot at getting clean and straightening your lives out. And why have we given you privileged young people one last chance?

4: Tell us.

SARGE: One reason is because you're special. You all have a drug problem, and you all committed your various acts of larceny to maintain a habit. In other words, your crimes were drug-related.

2: So why does that make us so special?

1: Yeah, what's up with this sh—, stuff. I feel like I'm in the Marines or something.

3: I never enlisted in no armed services.

SARGE: You people are special because in your young lives, you have rebelled against every system or structure you have come up against. You have rebelled against your family; you have rebelled against the school system; you have rebelled against society; and by developing a drug problem, you have even rebelled against yourselves.

4: Just call us rebels, man.

3: That's right.

2: Wait a minute. How do you rebel against yourself?

SARGE: By trying to kill yourself.

2: I ain't trying to kill myself. What are you talking about?

1: The drugs, man. He's talking about the drugs.

SARGE: You got it. This place may look like boot camp, but it's really one of the most sophisticated drug rehabilitation programs in the state.

4: What are you going to do to us, man?

SARGE: We are going to tell you when to get up in the morning. When to go to bed at night. What to eat. When to go to the bathroom. When to breathe. And when not to breathe. Essentially, we are going to control every aspect of your lives because up until now, you haven't been doing a very good job of that yourselves.

2: That's intense.

SARGE: (*Pointing to a building at the opposite end of the field*) Do you all see that building way down there? I want you all to sprint there on the whistle.

4: What are you talking about? You want me to run?

SARGE: You got it.

4: What for?

SARGE: You all got an appointment at the beauty parlor. We're gonna make you all beautiful.

3: Not hair cuts?

SARGE: Short ones.

2: How short?

SARGE: (*Smiling*) Real short.

4: Oh, no.

1: Oh, sh—

SARGE: (*Interrupting for the last time*) Move out!

They all begin to jog reluctantly toward the building in the distance.

Discussion

1. Describe the similarities between a military boot camp and this drug rehabilitation center. What might be the reasoning behind making the two so similar?

2. Do you think this approach would be successful? Explain.

3. Why does the Sarge say that 1,2,3, and 4 are trying to kill themselves? Do you agree?

4. Would you put up with a program like this or would you rather do your time in prison? Explain.

5. What would this program do for drug abusers that prison might not?

The Faculty Meeting

Topic
drug testing of teachers

Characters
Jim Feeney, Principal of Hope High School
Ms. Rose, Director of Health Services for the school
Three vocal teachers

FEENEY *addresses the faculty of Hope High School.*
It is the first faculty meeting of the year.

FEENEY: Welcome back, everyone. I'm sure that after the summer break you are all eager to be back at school. (*General moans and groans*) Come on, it's not all that bad, is it? (*Louder moans and groans*) Well, perhaps we should move on to our first agenda item. If you would all turn to the agenda you received at the beginning of the meeting, you will see that item number one concerns "change in working conditions."

TEACHER 1: Jim, have you notified the union yet? Any change in working conditions is strictly against the present contract.

FEENEY: Well, let me first explain the change, and then we will discuss its legality or illegality.

TEACHER 3: Why are you wasting everyone's time? *Any* change in working conditions will—

FEENEY: Please. Let me just address the issue, and then we will address your concerns. As you are all aware, at the close of school last year we had two students overdose on drugs in one of the lavatories.

TEACHER 2: How are they doing?

TEACHER 1: Any word?

FEENEY: Physically, they are both fine. Their families have decided to place them both in treatment centers, and they may be returning to school sometime around Christmas. (*General relief and approval from the staff*) However, that tragic incident brought to light a painfully serious subject we are facing in this community and in this school: the growing problem of drug and alcohol abuse.

TEACHER 3: It's about time we hit this problem head on. I had too many kids in class stoned last year.

TEACHER 2: And drunk.

TEACHER 1: That's right!

FEENEY: We are all well aware of the increase in the problem. That's why, over the summer, a committee of community members, school board members, and school administrators was formed. The committee's specific task was to stop the spread of this "cancer."

TEACHER 2: Terrific!

TEACHER 3: What conclusions did you come up with?

FEENEY: Well, for the specifics, I would like to pass the microphone to Celia Rose. She will be instrumental in instituting the committee's changes. Celia.

ROSE: Thanks, Jim. Hi, everyone. I'm glad to hear you are all aware that this problem has gotten out of control. You see it in your classes. You see it in the halls. You see it in the community. I'm sure you will join with us to do anything we can to put a stop to it. (*General agreement*) Great. Let me tell you first that at the class assemblies on Wednesday, we will be announcing the institution of a school-wide drug testing program.

TEACHER 1: That's great!

TEACHER 3: Terrific.

TEACHER 2: It's about time these kids are held accountable.

ROSE: The students will be brought to the gym after each assembly, and, under the supervision of the school doctor and her assistants, urine will be taken. It will then be tested. You will find a specific description of the entire process, including treatment and penalties, on page thirty-three of your handbook.

The teachers all turn to page thirty-three. After a minute or so, a growing mumble can be heard from the audience.

TEACHER 1: Hey, everyone, turn to page thirty-seven!

TEACHER 2: What is this? Mandatory *teacher* drug tests?

TEACHER 3: This is bull.

ROSE: This is the change in working conditions that Jim alluded to at the beginning of the meeting.

TEACHER 3: You can't do this!

ROSE: We can and we have.

TEACHER 2: Does the union know about this?

ROSE: It does now.

TEACHER 1: This is illegal!

ROSE: That is up to the courts to decide. As of today, every teacher in this district is required to take mandatory random urine tests throughout the school year.

General mayhem erupts.

TEACHER 1: We refuse!

TEACHER 2: This is an invasion of our privacy.

ROSE: This is an attempt to curb the drug problem in this school.

TEACHER 3: But we're teachers!

ROSE: Exactly. You should be setting an example for your students. If the teachers are held accountable through drug tests, the committee felt that the students would be more likely to comply. What's the problem? Do any of you have anything to hide?

More general mayhem ensues.

TEACHER 1: That's not the issue, and you know it. We should be judged on our performance in the classroom, not on our personal lives.

ROSE: But if you were all serious about solving this problem with drugs and alcohol, you should be glad to participate in the testing.

FEENEY: That's right. You're professionals, aren't you?

TEACHER 2: We are professionals, and we are concerned, but we refuse to sit here and let out constitutional rights be violated.

TEACHER 1: That's right. We're outta here.

TEACHER 3: Come on, people. We need to have a little meeting ourselves—at the union office.

TEACHER 1: Let's go!

The teachers get up en masse and leave the faculty meeting as the principal tries to remind them of their contractual duties.

FEENEY: Wait. This meeting isn't over. Please, stay in your seats. Please...

Discussion

1. Do you think that teachers should be tested for drug and alcohol abuse? Explain.

2. Do you think students should be tested? Explain.

3. Which professions do you think should or shouldn't be tested for drug and alcohol abuse?

4. Do you think that this type of testing infringes upon a person's civil liberties? Explain.

The Senior Assembly

Topic
drug testing of students

Characters
Mr. Feeney, Principal of Hope High School
Ms. Rose, Director of Health Services for the school
Three vocal students

> FEENEY *and* ROSE *are addressing the senior class of Hope High School. It is the first of four meetings planned for this student group.*

FEENEY: Welcome back, everyone. I'm sure that after the summer break you are all eager to be back at school.

> *There are general groans and moans from the crowd.*

Come on, it's not all that bad, is it?

> *The crowd groans and moans louder.*

Well, perhaps we should move on to our next topic. Let's see. We have Ms. Duff, your class advisor, up here. In a few minutes, she is going to introduce you to your class reps and talk to you about fund raising for the prom. We also have Mr. Johns here to talk to you about hall passes and going off campus for lunch, something that you all know is strictly against policy.

The crowd again moans and groans.

But before we get to those speakers, I would like to discuss a serious issue with all of you because you are all seniors and you are all familiar with the things we have done in this school to confront the problems of drug and alcohol abuse. We have growing participation in SADD and members of the PTA have just started a community-wide MADD program. We have included guest lectures in our health classes on drugs and substance abuse, and we have cooperated with the local police to crack down on dealers in our community. Unfortunately, all of our efforts do not seem to be sufficient. Last June, during exam week, we had two students overdose in the bathroom. Thank God they pulled through. And we have had more and more *students* arrested for selling drugs on school property than ever before. The administration is concerned about this rise in apparent drug abuse, and the community is also concerned. Over the summer, a committee was formed to confront this problem. They have made several important changes in how things are run in the school. To explain the most important change, I would like to introduce Ms. Rose, the Director of Health Services. Ms. Rose.

ROSE: Thank you, Mr. Feeney. Before I begin, I want you all to understand that we all believe drug and alcohol abuse among high school students is perhaps the greatest problem this school faces. We cannot allow the problem to spiral out of control, so we have taken some serious steps to stop it. The first step we have taken is that we have instituted mandatory drug testing for all students, effective immediately.

The seniors react in an uproar.

STUDENT 1: *(Calling)* What do you mean?

STUDENT 2: What kind of drug testing?

STUDENT 3: This is against the law!

FEENEY: *(Taking the microphone from ROSE)* Calm down. Please. Calm down. If you just let Ms. Rose talk, all of your questions will be answered.

STUDENT 3: *(Calling out and still irate)* Isn't mandatory drug testing against the law?

ROSE: No. The courts have ruled that school districts and individual schools run according to the rules of those individual schools, communities, and administrators. Contrary to popular belief, high schools are not democracies. If we feel that student lives are in danger, we can search lockers. We can search purses. We can search individuals, and we can impose mandatory drug testing.

Loud disapproval erupts from the audience.

STUDENT 1: What type of drug testing are you talking about?

ROSE: After this assembly, you will all report to the gym. We have set up teams that include the school doctor and his assistants to monitor the collection of urine from each student. The urine will then be tested, and the results will go to the nurse, the administration, and your parents.

STUDENT 2: What if we refuse?

STUDENT 3: Students who are absent or who refuse to provide urine under supervision will be given one other opportunity to comply. If a student fails to take advantage of the second opportunity, then we have been given the authority by the State Education Department to suspend you from classes until you comply.

STUDENT 1: What if the tests show that we have used drugs?

STUDENT 3: What are you going to do, arrest us?

ROSE: No. You will not be arrested. If a student's urine test indicates the presence of drugs in the system, we will schedule another test immediately. If that second test shows the presence of drugs in the system, we will arrange a meeting between the student, his or her parents, an administrator, and the school nurse. That student will have to take part in a special drug education and treatment program that the school has established. The student's urine will be monitored weekly for a period of six months. If the student remains drug-free for six months, he or she is removed from the program. If drugs appear in the student's urine at any time, the student will have to remain in the program, and further steps will have to be taken to insure that the student remains drug-free.

STUDENT 3: This sucks!

STUDENT 2: It's ridiculous!

STUDENT 1: It's like a dictatorship!

ROSE: We must make sure that you people don't kill yourselves with illegal substances.

STUDENT 1: What about our rights.?

ROSE: When you are in this school and when it comes to drug testing, you have none.

The crowd voices general disapproval.

STUDENT 2: But we're seniors! We are seventeen and eighteen years old! We're adults. Shouldn't we be able to do what we want with our own bodies? Shouldn't we be able to take care of ourselves?

ROSE: Unfortunately, up until now, many of you have not been able to take care of yourselves. You have not been able to make the right decisions. So, we have decided to make the right decisions for you.

FEENEY: (*Stepping back up to the microphone*) That's right, and I'm afraid the time for discussion is over. If you want to remain in this school, you must comply. Listen, it's done in the business world every day. I don't know what your problem is.

STUDENT 3: I'll tell you what our problem is. You just—

FEENEY: (*Cutting the student off*) I'm sorry, but the assembly is running late. We have to move on to Ms. Duff and fund raising. Ms. Duff.

Discussion

1. What will happen to those students who do not comply with the drug testing program?

2. Do you think this process is fair? Explain.

3. Comment on the statement, "High schools are not democracies."

4. How would you feel if this program were instituted in your school? Would you comply? Explain.

The Parent Group #3

Topic
the role of parents in preventing abuse

Characters
Dr. Lasky, the leader of a group of parents whose children are
  substance abusers
Parents in the group
  Mrs. Adams
  Mr. Oldham
  Mrs. Street
  Mr. Meier
  Mrs. Grace

DR. LASKY *is sitting on a couch in his office with the group of parents seated comfortably around him.*

DR. LASKY: Welcome, everybody. I know that the first meeting of any group is uncomfortable, so I thought that I would take tonight's session to explain how this process works and to give you some background information.

MR. OLDHAM: (*Not happy to be there*) What sort of background information?

DR. LASKY: Hold on, Mr. Oldham. We're jumping ahead. First let me lay the ground rules. You are all here today because you share a problem. Each of you has an adolescent child who is abusing or has abused drugs. Many of you are here or has abused drugs. Many of you are here because you have recognized the problem and have decided that you need some help in dealing with it. A few of you are here because a family court judge has decided that counseling for the parent is just as important as counseling for the teenage abuser.

MR. OLDHAM: My daughter's the one who is hooked on crack, not me.

DR. LASKY: I know, I know, Mr. Oldham. And with any luck, we will all help *you* help *her*.

MR. OLDHAM: (*Annoyed*) Whatever.

MRS. GRACE: What is this background information you were talking about, doctor?

DR. LASKY: Well, I usually begin these sessions with some hard core statistics that may amaze you.

MRS. ADAMS: Like what?

DR. LASKY: In my experience, the average parent these days doesn't really know that much about drugs. Kids are getting educated about drugs in school now, but they're getting no reinforcement at home. Parents just don't know the facts.

MR. OLDHAM: What facts?

DR. LASKY: For instance, did you know that a survey of high school kids in 1993 stated that about sixty-six percent of students from grades seven to twelve used alcohol in the past year, twenty-three percent used tobacco, fourteen percent used marijuana, 5.9 percent used hallucinogens, and 2.7 percent used cocaine?

MRS. STREETER: I can't believe that a child in the seventh grade would know where to get cocaine let alone how to use it.

you stop and think about how many children that may include, the number is staggering.

MR. MEIER: But, Dr. Lasky, what good will knowing these statistics do for us? My son is not interested in percentages!

DR. LASKY: There is no evidence that well-informed parents raise children who stay away from drugs, but experts are convinced that by educating parents we will also be helping children. We do know that our local treatment center has told us that well-informed parents at least know what signs of substance abuse to look for in their children. They're better able to recognize if their child has a problem.

MR. OLDHAM: (*Sarcastically*) My child has a problem all right.

DR. LASKY: Research has also told us that good parenting may be the best prevention of adolescent substance abuse.

MR. OLDHAM: What are you trying to say?

DR. LASKY: What I am saying, Mr. Oldham, is that creating an atmosphere where children feel free to talk about drugs and setting a good example are among the best tools a parent can use to raise a drug-free kid.

MRS. GRACE: Then aren't you saying that it's too late for us, Dr. Lasky? After all, we are here because our kids have already developed drug problems. Why are we all here sitting around wasting our time?

DR. LASKY: I hope that you will not be wasting your time, Mrs. Grace. But you are all here because doing nothing is very, very dangerous.

MRS. GRACE: Then tell us what to do!

DR. LASKY: I'm afraid it's not that simple. But I'll tell you what I *am* going to do. I am going to let each of *you* tell us what to do.

The group emits general murmurs of objection.

MR. OLDHAM: Hey, listen, doc, if we knew what to do, we wouldn't all be sitting here listening to you.

DR. LASKY: I'm through talking. Unfortunately, the most effective solutions and the most reasonable answers to problems such as yours come from people who have paid the highest price. In the sessions to come, you are each going to tell us your own particular story of your own particular child. Mrs. Adams?

MRS. ADAMS: Yes?

DR. LASKY: Do you still want to be the first one?

MRS. ADAMS: Sure.

MRS. STREETER: Wait a minute. No body told me that I would have to tell anybody anything. My life is my business, and I don't want to share it with complete strangers.

DR. LASKY: No one is going to force you to do anything, Mrs. Streeter. But I'm sure that after this group hears what happened to Benny Adams last August, you will not feel like strangers any more. Unfortunately, our time is up for tonight. I'll see you all next week.

Discussion

1. How can you tell that Mr. Oldham is resentful that he is attending group therapy?

2. Do you think that Mr. Oldham has the right to feel resentful? Explain.

3. Do you think Mr. Oldham should leave the group? Explain.

4. What do experts believe about educating parents about drugs?

5. Do you think that these sessions will be helpful? Explain.

The Assembly

Topic
teenagers and alcohol

Characters
Recovering teenage alcoholics who speak to elementary students
  Scott
  Mary
  Allison
Mr. Parks, a fifth-grade teacher
Four vocal students in an audience of about forty fifth-grade children

> SCOTT, MARY, *and* ALLISON *are on the stage of an elementary school. They are speaking to two classes of fifth-graders about drinking and alcoholism. Their audience is seated on the floor in front of the stage.* PARKS, *one of the fifth-grade teachers, introduces them.*

PARKS: All right people, settle down. We are lucky today to have three students from the high school who have come to talk to you all about alcohol and alcoholism. How many of you have parents who drink alcohol?

> *Almost every hand raises.*

How many of you have older brothers and sisters who drink alcohol?

> *Again, the same response.*

Well, Allison, Mary, and Scott are going to tell you a few things to look out for. Please give them your complete attention.

PARKS *goes into the audience as* ALLISON *comes to the microphone.*

ALLISON: Hey, you guys. I'm Allison. How are you all doing?

The crowd responds with a general murmur of "Hello."

You guys are in the fifth grade, aren't you?

They murmur "Yes."

I remember when I was in the fifth grade. Let's see, how old was I? Ten. Are most of you guys ten?

Again, a general murmur of "Yes."

I remember fifth grade real well because that was the year my brother died. I'm here today to tell you that story. Now listen, I get really upset sometimes when I tell it, so if I have to stop once or twice, I want you to understand why. Here goes. When I was in fifth grade, I was living with my brother, Kevin. He was twenty-four. He was into drinking big time. I was home by myself one day when he came in and fell on the floor. He was drunk again. The friends that were with him put him on the couch. After a few minutes, they told me to call an ambulance. Because we didn't have a phone, I ran to my neighbor's apartment and called my grandmother and the police. When I came back, one of his friends was screaming, "He's dead! He's dead!" I ran in and said that he wasn't dead. He was just drunk again. Then I went over and looked at him. He was purple. I tried doing CPR on him but nothing worked. When the ambulance came, I knew he was dead. The people at the hospital said that he had drowned himself in alcohol. (*Getting upset*) He was my big brother, and I miss him. That happened when I was in fifth grade, but I remember it like it was yesterday.

SCOTT *comes to the microphone to give* ALLISON *a hug.* ALLISON *takes her seat on stage as* SCOTT *begins to talk to the fifth graders.*

SCOTT: I didn't lose a brother like Allison did, but I almost lost my own life. Hi, my name is Scott, and I started drinking when I was twelve years old. My parents never knew, and I was smart enough in school to drink and still pass all my classes. I thought that I had it made until last year when I was a junior. My two friends and I drank about four six-packs one Friday night. We were feeling pretty good until my friend Mickey started to drive us home. We almost made it when he missed a turn and slammed into a telephone pole at about seventy miles an hour. My two friends were killed. I just broke my leg. I haven't had a drink since that night, and I'm here to tell you that it all began when I was in sixth grade. Did you know that alcohol is America's number one drug problem among young people and that there are about thirty-three million teenage alcoholics in this country today? And listen to this: Kids who are in kindergarten today will have seen one hundred thousand beer commercials by the time they graduate from high school. Those are just some numbers to think about. Now, I'd like to introduce to Mary.

SCOTT *sits down and* MARY *takes the microphone.*

MARY: Hi, everybody. Unlike Allison and Scott, I'm not going to tell you my own story, even though, trust me, I have a good one. But what I would like you to do now is think about your own lives. Like Mr. Parks did at the beginning of the assembly, I'm going to ask you if you have any stories you would like to share about alcohol. (*She waits for a hand to be raised as the audience talks nervously to themselves.*) Anyone have a story to share? It can be about anything.

STUDENT 1: I tasted scotch once and almost threw up. (*Audience laughs*) Why would anyone want to drink that stuff?

MARY: I have no idea. Anyone else?

STUDENT 2: One of my dad's friends left a Super Bowl party and drove off the road at one hundred miles an hour and was killed.

MARY: Wow, that's awful. Was your dad really upset?

STUDENT 2: Yeah.

STUDENT 3: My dad always makes me get in the car with him after he's had too much to drink. Isn't that supposed to be dangerous?

MARY: It sure is.

STUDENT 3: But what can I do? He's my dad. I have to do what he says.

MARY: You have to listen to your dad but not when you think he is doing something that you think could hurt you or could hurt him. The next time it happens, tell your mother or your grandfather or your older sister. Tell somebody. They'll help you stop it.

STUDENT 4: (*Quietly*) My brother is a drunk. I know he is. What can I do?

ALLISON: (*From her seat*) You can get him help, so he doesn't die like mine did! What's your name?

STUDENT 4: Jeffrey.

ALLISON: Jeffrey, I want to talk to you when this is over, okay?

STUDENT 4: Okay.

PARKS *gets up from the audience and mounts the stage.*

PARKS: Well, I'm afraid that that's all the time we have for today. Can we all thank our guests from the high school for coming over? (*Applause*) If anyone would like to speak with Allison, Mary, or Scott, just come up to the stage, and I'm sure they would be glad to talk. Thanks, everyone! You were a great audience.

Discussion

1. Do you think that fifth graders are too young to talk to about problems involving alcohol?

2. Is the sharing of personal stories an effective way to educate younger children about alcohol?

3. Do you know any younger children who have been affected by alcohol abuse? How do you think you could help them?

4. What stories of your own concerning alcohol could you relate?

No

Topic
refusing alcohol or other drugs

Characters
Narrator
Voices 1 and 2, voices of temptation
Voices 3 and 4, voices that say "No"

> *The audience hears four disembodied voices.*

NARRATOR: It's tough to say "No" and mean it. I know, you've all heard the slogan, "Just say no." But what they don't tell you is that it's pretty hard to turn down a beer or a joint and not look like a jerk. After all, we have images to maintain and girls to impress and boyfriends to flirt with. If we come off looking like we're too good to drink a beer or above smoking a joint, we think we are going to wind up with very few friends. Listen to how some people handle the pressure.

1: Hey, do you smoke?

3: No. Not really, thanks.

2: Come on, one hit won't hurt you.

4: No, no thanks.

1: Come on.

178

3: Listen, I'm doing spring track, and that stuff just kills my lungs.

4: You know, I have asthma and any smoke makes me gag.

2: But it's a party.

4: I've got a major test tomorrow.

1: Forget about it. Have some fun.

3: I just don't smoke, okay?

4: I'm still getting over this cold, and I feel lousy.

1: What's the matter, you're too cool to get stoned or something?

4: Listen, I don't need to smoke pot to be cool.

3: My brother would kill me.

1: Hey, I'm not gonna tell anybody. Are you?

2: Yeah, you're responsible for your own life. Are you a dweeb or something?

4: I have my dad's car. I don't need any accidents.

2: Why don't you live a little?

4: That's what I'm trying to do.

1: What's that?

2: What did you say?

1, 2: I don't get it.

3: Get off my back.

4: Get a life.

3: Get lost.

4: Get real.

3: Get away from me.

3, 4: Now.

Discussion

1. Do you have the right to say "No"? Explain.

2. What are some polite ways of saying "No" that you have used?

3. What should you do if someone refuses to take "No" for an answer?

Responsibility

Topic
accepting responsibility for substance abuse problems

Characters
1, a parent
2, a teacher
3, a teenager

> *All three characters speak directly to the audience.*

ALL: I'm not responsible.

1: He's out of control. How do you expect me to do anything about him?

2: You should see what I see.

3: I'm just a kid, man.

1: Ever since my husband left, it's just been me. I can't raise three kids all by myself.

3: My mom is never home. It's not her fault. She's got to pay the rent. I'm left pretty much on my own.

2: Do you know how many kids I have in my classes? You can't expect me to reach every one of them. Besides, I teach English. I'm not a social worker.

3: I got to watch my brothers and sisters most afternoons because my mom doesn't get home until about six. But when she gets home, I take off. She never asks where I'm going because one, she's too busy, and two, she knows that I watched the kids all afternoon, and she wants to give me a break.

1: It's not like I want to work. It's not like I want him to watch his sisters. But what do you expect me to do? Someone has got to put food on the table.

2: When I call the house, I always get the answering machine. Aren't his parents ever home? It's not as though I have never tried to contact them.

3: It's not my mother's fault that I'm so messed up. She's doing her best. She works hard.

1: He's really a good boy. He helps out as much as he can. I guess he's just hanging out with the wrong crowd.

2: I try to talk to him in class, but he never wants to stay after the bell. I want to ask him why he's sleeping in my class. Every day he puts his head down about halfway through class. I just don't understand.

3: I just don't understand why the school is getting on my case. I show up. I'm never absent. So I don't do all the work. Big deal. I got other things to do.

2: I suspect that he's using drugs. But I can't prove it.

1: This teacher left a message on the answering machine saying she wanted to talk to me. I know what she's going to say. What does she want me to do about it?

3: So I drink some beer and get stoned. I need a break, too. I watch the kids all afternoon. I show up for school. You can't blame me for wanting to party with my friends, can you?

1: His friends are always so polite when they come to the house or call him on the phone. They sound like nice kids. I can't believe that they are involved with drugs. I can't believe that my son would get involved with people like that.

2: I'm getting very concerned about the situation.

3: I'm starting to black out sometimes from drinking so much.

1: Now I can see that something is wrong. He's acting differently. All he wants to do is sleep all day.

ALL: I better get a handle on this.

2: I better speak to someone.

1: I better talk to him.

3: I better get a grip. Things are starting to get nasty.

Discussion

1. List three reasons why each character does not feel responsible for the trouble the teenager is getting into.

2. Are these reasons legitimate?

3. Describe the teenager's family situation. Doesn't he have the right to some free time after being given so much responsibility at home?

4. What could each character have done to have prevented the teenager from getting too involved with drugs and drinking?

5. Do you know any teenagers in similar situations? How do they handle the extra family responsibility? Have they turned to drugs or alcohol? Why or why not?

Index of Topics

More Skits and Activities

ACTING IT OUT: 174 Short Plays for Starting Discussions with Teenagers
Joan Sturkie & Marsh Cassady, PhD

Paper, 358 pages, 6" x 9", ISBN 0-89390-178-4

Getting teens to talk about their feelings and personal experiences can be frustrating. *Acting It Out* offers a new approach: Teens act out a short play, then discuss how the characters deal with the particular issue. Questions at the end of each drama help students articulate feelings. These dramas address challenging subjects such as abortion, suicide, child abuse, gangs, anorexia, home life, drugs. Issues are presented in a straightforward manner and your teens are encouraged to talk about them in the same way.

FACING VIOLENCE: Discussion-Starting Skits for Teenagers
R. William Pike

Paper, 6" x 9", 192 pages, ISBN 0-89390-344-2

Teens have many reasons for acting up. Trouble at home. Trouble with relationships. Trouble on the streets. You can get them to talk about their problems and explore solutions by using simple dramas. *Facing Violence*, part of the ACTING IT OUT series, provides you with 40 skits addressing violence in schools, violence in the home, violent language, violence and dating, violence and bias, violence in society—and solutions. Try them. They work!

STREET SMARTS: Activities That Help Teenagers Take Care of Themselves
Dr. Michael Kirby

Paper, 80 pages, 8½" x 11", ISBN 0-89390-331-0

Growing up, teenagers start out in the relatively secure environment of home and school. Somehow they must learn how to make it in the more hazardous world of work and adulthood. They have to learn how to take care of themselves. This book examines the many roadblocks in their way and helps them explore how to overcome them. Case studies, role-plays, and activities involve them in the process and make the learning fun. A great resource for a variety of classrooms and small groups. Could be used as a course or as pick-and-choose activities. Includes permission to photocopy student handouts.

Order from your local bookseller, or contact:

 Resource Publications, Inc.
160 E. Virginia Street #290
San Jose, CA 95112-5876
1-800-736-7600 (voice)
1-408-287-8748 (fax)
http://www.rpinet.com